# Facing the Storm

We live in a world where bad things can, and do, happen irrespective of whether we are good or bad, whether we consider ourselves lucky or doomed, and with no regard to fairness. Any of us can find ourselves facing redundancy, the breakdown of a relationship, bankruptcy or any number of life-changing crises, or supporting someone else who is. And sometimes, no matter how much we might try, there's nothing we can do to prevent or reduce the problem.

But that doesn't mean you have to be helpless; no matter how bad the situation you're about to deal with, there are things that you can do to become more resilient and that will help you face the storm that's coming towards you or yours.

Using cognitive behavioural therapy (CBT) techniques and the latest developments in mindfulness and acceptance-based approaches, this practical guide will take you through each stage of preparing for, enduring and recovering from a major life crisis, helping you better understand what's going on, and providing new tools for dealing with the situation.

When there's a storm coming towards you, and you can't escape it, then you have to prepare to face it. Here's how.

**Dr Ray Owen** is a clinical psychologist working in cancer and palliative care for the NHS in Herefordshire. He has worked in hospital, community and hospice settings for the past 20 years.

# Facing the Storm

## Using CBT, mindfulness and acceptance to build resilience when your world's falling apart

*Ray Owen*

Routledge
Taylor & Francis Group

LONDON AND NEW YORK

First published 2011
by Routledge
27 Church Road, Hove, East Sussex BN3 2FA

Simultaneously published in the USA and Canada
by Routledge
711 Third Avenue, New York NY 10017

*Routledge is an imprint of the Taylor & Francis Group, an Informa business*

*British Library Cataloguing in Publication Data*
A catalogue record for this book is available from the British Library

*Library of Congress Cataloging in Publication Data*
Owen, Ray, 1964-
  Facing the storm : using CBT, mindfulness and acceptance to build
resilience when your world's falling apart / Ray Owen.
     p. cm.
  Includes bibliographical references and index.
  ISBN 978-0-415-67658-8 (hbk.) – ISBN 978-0-415-67659-5 (pbk.)
  1. Life change events. 2. Adjustment (Psychology) 3. Cognitive therapy. 4.
Mindfulness-based cognitive therapy. I. Title.
  BF637.L53O94 2011
  158–dc22

                                                          2011007014

ISBN: 978-0-415-67658-8 (hbk)
ISBN: 978-0-415-67659-5 (pbk)
ISBN: 978-0-203-80555-8 (ebk)

Typeset in New Century Schoolbook by Garfield Morgan,
Swansea, West Glamorgan
Printed and bound in Great Britain by TJ International Ltd
Padstow, Cornwall
Cover design by Andrew Ward

# Dedication

To Ronya, Sam and Tim, for their patience and support

# Contents

# Preface

When Jeff sat down in my office, I could see that the cancer and the chemotherapy had taken a toll in the month since we'd last met. His clothes were looking too big on him, his posture was more slouched than before and his voice was weaker. Yet I couldn't forget that this was a man who, a year earlier, had been exceptionally fit and robust, and had looked at least ten years younger than his actual age of 67. He was ex-army, and had spent most of his life travelling, bringing up his family on a succession of different continents, as often on boats as on land. He must have been feeling very rough to have agreed to visit a doctor at all, and when his cancer was diagnosed, he had thrown himself into the treatment with the same commitment he brought to everything else in life.

We'd met a few times (reluctantly on his part at first) because he'd found the shock of being physically limited and dependent on others hard to bear. Once he'd realised I wasn't going to make him lie on a couch and talk about his potty-training, but instead look at practical ways of coping with his situation and his mood swings, we got on well and he quickly regained his usual bullish confidence.

Now I was seeing him because he'd had more bad news; the initial treatment hadn't worked, and it looked as if the cancer wasn't going to be held back; sadly, he was unlikely to live more than a small number of months.

Understandably, he was devastated; he was scared of what lay ahead, didn't know whether to rush around trying to fight the inevitable, or just lie down and wait for the end.

He said it reminded him of an experience years before: he and his wife had been crewing a sailing yacht around some Pacific islands for people who wanted the ultimate getaway cruise. During the off-season, they were staying at a beach-front house on a sparsely populated island. One day, he heard a gale warning over the radio; storms were common enough during that season, but apparently a full-blown tropical cyclone was heading their way. There was no time to get off the island safely, so a direct hit looked pretty much inevitable.

Jeff said that it was the same now – you can see disaster coming, and coming soon, but there's not a damn thing you can do to stop it (though he didn't say 'damn' . . .), and you feel overwhelmed and helpless.

'So what *did* you do?' I asked him.

'I froze at first.'

'And then?'

'And then I started getting ready for the storm.'

'OK; so that's what we're going to do now . . .'

A little while later, I was talking to Patricia, a recent widow, who had struggled to cope with the loss of her husband. Her own health was failing, and without his support, it was becoming obvious that she wouldn't be able to manage in her own home for much longer. Yet the loss of that house and all its memories, as well as her independence, felt like the end of the world. She knew that leaving was unavoidable, and the time was coming closer. How, she asked tearfully, could anyone live with that hanging over their head?

As so often, I felt some of her hopelessness washing over me too; but then I remembered Jeff – facing his cyclone, and now facing his death, but not just lying down and waiting for them to happen.

'Well, Patricia, though that's a huge loss ahead of you, there are some things you could do to help you face it . . .'

# Acknowledgements

My first thanks must go to all the patients and their families from whom I've learned so much that has ended up in this book. Though none of them appears directly, the lessons, anecdotes and case histories are informed by their experiences.

I would also like to acknowledge the many colleagues of various professions whom I have worked with. While some of the techniques in this book have evolved specifically within my own practice, others are standard things that are being done all the time in different settings throughout the country. Credit for them rests in part with the innovative researchers and teachers who write the books and papers we read, and especially those involved in the development of the 'third wave' therapies including Dr Jon Kabat-Zinn, Professor Mark Williams, Professor Steve Hayes and Dr Russ Harris. It also rests with the workface psychologists, psychiatrists, counsellors, nurses, doctors and so on who further develop those techniques, come up with novel ways of doing things and saying them, and then share these tips with colleagues. I hope anyone reading this book as 'work' will find one or two new ideas they want to include in their own toolbox.

I would also like to thank those who have read prior drafts of this book, and been kind enough to offer detailed and constructive comments, notably Sian James, Cath Stewart, Dr David Jeffrey, Kate Jones, Dave Price and most thoroughly of all, my wife, Ronya. Any inaccuracies or omissions remaining in the text, though, are entirely my own responsibility.

# Storms happen

## Introduction

We live in a world where bad things can, and do, happen. To all of us and potentially at any time of our lives, irrespective of whether we are good or bad, whether we consider ourselves lucky or doomed, and with no regard to fairness.

Of course, it makes no sense to walk around our whole lives constantly thinking about this, and living in ongoing dread of the next disaster.

But there come points in our lives when we know something bad is going to happen, and fairly soon – the storm's on the horizon and heading our way. Maybe the relationship you've tried to keep alive is irrevocably breaking down. Or your company is in trouble, there will be redundancies, and you'll be one of them. Perhaps you're facing legal action – jail even. There are a million possibilities, including (arguably worst of all) that someone you love is very ill, and will soon die.

Although the details of each of these events differ, they have some things in common: life is likely to change for the worse, it is likely to be stressful while the event is happening, there is nothing (now) you can do to prevent the catastrophe, and there may well be important details (including the exact timing of the event) which you cannot be sure of. In these ways, it resembles the storm that Jeff was waiting for (see Preface).

It's well established that this combination of highly unpleasant events, uncertainty and little control over them is a recipe for high levels of stress and difficulty in functioning.[1] And there is no approach, no therapy or self-help manual that can make all of this OK.

So are we to be passive victims in the face of the disasters that life throws at us? Not necessarily, for even when something is very far from OK, or from what we would have ever chosen, some people seem able to function better, remain less stressed, more able to make sense of their situation and make necessary decisions; in short, they *cope* better. But these people aren't just born 'copers' who will sail through life while the rest of us are doomed to struggle. Put someone who coped well in one situation into a different crisis, and they may find themselves as helpless as any of us.

Why? Because it's not some lifelong personality trait that makes a person able to cope, but how they *react* in a given situation; how they look at things, what they say to themselves or others, how they act. If these approaches don't match a new situation, that person may not cope so well this time.

Now, the good news in this is that we can learn to react in those ways ourselves to deal with the situations that we face. We can learn to be more resilient.

You might object that all this kind of thing might be useful for facing the 'smaller stuff' of life – tricky times at work, disappointing exam results, but surely not when facing the kind of major catastrophes mentioned above? Let me show why that's not true.

There's an area of healthcare called 'palliative care'; it involves doctors, nurses, psychologists, social workers and a whole range of other professionals working in hospitals, hospices and people's homes. The goal is to support those who have an illness which cannot be cured and will ultimately lead to their death – typically cancer, heart failure, motor neurone disease or other degenerative conditions. At the very core of this approach is the acceptance that something bad is indeed going to happen, there's nothing that can be done to prevent it, but the details of exactly how and when the disease will progress will be unpredictable.

Helen is a 49-year-old mother of two; she has a 29-year-old daughter, Emma, from her first marriage (which ended when Emma was small). She has been in a stable relationship with Keith for many years now, and they have an 8-year-old son, Liam.

She has suffered from stomach problems of different sorts for years, putting many of them down to her stressful life as a care worker at a local residential home. After a particularly bad bout of digestive problems, she returns to her family doctor, who sends her for investigations at the hospital. Within a few days, she is called back to see the consultant, who tells her that she has advanced bowel cancer, which looks as if it has already spread to other organs. Sadly, it will not be curable; a variety of treatments might slow down further spread of the disease and/or help manage its symptoms, but it will inevitably advance further, ultimately leading to her death.

Helen's case, though fictional, is typical of the kind of situation where palliative care becomes involved. At one time, people like her might have been told by the doctors that 'there's nothing more we can do'. In palliative care, there's always something we can do, and we don't give up; but our goal isn't unrealistic hope of a miracle cure, rather it's of getting the best possible symptom control, care and support, as well as help with making family, social or even legal arrangements. In short, to achieve the best quality of life possible under the circumstances. And the psychological element is in supporting the patients and their families in coping with the situation as best they can; making sense of what is happening, adjusting to the changes, making the decisions required, planning as much as possible despite the uncertainties, and dealing with the emotional impact of the whole situation.

So, even when facing your own death, or the death of someone you love, there are ways of coping better.

I have spent nearly twenty years as a clinical psychologist in palliative care specialising in helping people cope with life-threatening illness. I use a variety of approaches, including cognitive behavioural therapy (CBT) and recent developments of it including mindfulness and acceptance-based techniques. I've seen time and again that they can work for people; but I've also noticed something else. Some of the people I see aren't imminently facing their own or a loved one's death, but are living (as best they can) a normal life for the time being. And some will come back and report that the ideas we've worked on for coping with death also help with other problems – a disciplinary hearing, a work crisis, a child leaving home.

And that's the message of this book: the things that can help a person face the biggest of events – death – can also be useful in facing other crises that come along. Even though these other events may not always be so bad as a death, they can still cause devastation within a person's life, or their family's.

It's important to be clear what I'm *not* saying: that negative events can always be avoided, that they can be rendered 'OK', and perish the thought that we should see everything as opportunities, not problems! On the contrary, the kinds of thing we're talking about are genuinely bad events, and deserve some respect for that. What I *am* saying is that in the face of major, inevitable, bad life events, a person can increase their understanding of the situation, increase their personal effectiveness, their quality of life and, in short, their coping.

This book is for anyone who is facing some kind of crisis, either immediately, or in their future. And that's all of us. But our main focus will be where it's fairly clear what's in store for you; like the Greek legend of Damocles, who looked up to see a sword dangling over his head, suspended by a single horse-hair, which could drop at any moment.[2] At the heart of our exploration will be this question: if you know that hair won't hold forever, how do you function, cope, deal with life and with the people around you? What we're about to discuss will also be useful to anyone facing less profound difficulties, or who is perhaps worried about how they would cope if (or when) they find themselves facing a crisis.

But major life events don't just happen to one person at a time; they involve the partner, the children, the friends, the colleagues. And if you're one of those people, you might end up struggling with both the direct impact on yourself, and also with knowing how to support the person in the middle of the crisis. So, what I have to say would apply to you too.

This book has two main aims: to help you make sense of what you are going through, and to present some of the strategies that can help – though, as we'll see, making sense of a situation is itself a key coping strategy. Remember, though, that in coping, as in clothing, it's rarely true that 'one size fits all' – that any particular example of the approaches in this book will suit everyone in every situation. After all, if you were receiving support from someone like a clinical psychologist, they would be working with you to produce a tailor-made approach that worked for you as an individual in your particular circumstances. By the end of the book, though, you'll have had the chance to look at your situation, think differently about it, and have access to a whole toolbox of techniques, at least some of which should suit you.

So each person's situation is unique, and you'll have to work out how best the ideas and techniques in this book apply to you. To give examples of ways that can work, we'll follow a group of people facing different life crises. The detail of the examples will be fictional, but they are based on real situations and real reactions I encounter.

I've already introduced Helen, who has just found out she has advanced cancer, and we'll return to her throughout the book to illustrate the ways that impending catastrophe can affect people, and how they can try to cope despite that. But we also need to look at how those same pressures and coping strategies apply to people facing other, non-cancer, crises.

Peter worked his way up through a medium-sized, family-owned printing company, to the point where he was effectively running the place. A few years ago the firm changed hands, and he started to get more and more frustrated that the new owners didn't listen to his advice as much as the old ones. This came to a head two years ago, when he was adamant that they were ignoring a potentially very profitable new niche in the market. With the support of his wife, Alice, he left his job shortly after his fiftieth birthday, remortgaged the family home and took out loans to start up his own company supplying this new market.

Business was slow to take off, and Peter had to take some additional loans to remain solvent until it picked up. Now, however, it's becoming clear to him that there isn't as much demand as he had thought, and that other, larger, companies have started offering the same service more cheaply. His business is failing, and he knows he will be unable to repay his debts, and will certainly lose the house. What's more, in his desperation to raise those extra loans in the first year, he misled the banks about his other commitments; when they find out, he thinks he will be facing fraud charges.

Anil (29) met his partner Sarah when they were both at college. They've lived together ever since, each pursuing their own careers and enjoying life in the city. Over time, though, Anil feels they've been growing apart; they've begun to differ on more things, from politics to redecoration, and crucially they cannot agree when (or whether) to start a family. Their social lives have become separate, with different groups of friends. Eighteen months ago, Sarah admitted to a brief affair with a colleague; this was a hugely stressful time for the couple, but they resolved to make the relationship work. Though he is still very much in love with Sarah, and is terrified of the prospect of life without her, Anil is realising that the relationship is drawing to an end. He can see Sarah's dissatisfaction, has evidence that she is having another affair, and is sure that she's about to leave him.

Debbie is 35 years old, a single mother with a 13-year-old daughter Beccy. Although she lives in an area of high unemployment, and didn't do well at school herself, she is (quite reasonably) proud of what she's achieved. She works as a highly skilled pattern-maker in a local textile company; while many jobs have been lost to automation, her specialist work has been irreplaceable. She isn't paid a fortune, but it was enough to allow her to get a mortgage on a small semi-detached house, she can take her daughter on holiday each year, and is even managing to save a little towards her going to college. These are opportunities she never had while growing up, and she is determined Beccy will have a better start in life. She's also a respected member of the local church group, and held up as a role model for other young single mums on the estate.

Then one day, Debbie hears that the parent company which owns her employer has decided to close down its entire UK operation, and transfer all activity to the Far East. Although no final date has been given, the closure looks certain. What's more, it was the last textile employer doing this kind of work in the region; there is no possibility of Debbie finding similar work nearby, and she realises that if she can get any work at all, it will be unskilled and very low paid. She will not be able to maintain mortgage payments, or carry on providing her daughter with those opportunities she promised she would give her.

As we say in palliative care: life can be really s\*\*t, can't it?

Although the crises faced by Peter, Anil and Debbie are not fatal like Helen's, they share the qualities of being major life events, apparently inevitable, but with uncertainty about exactly when and how these bad things are going to happen. There's going to be no last-minute reprieve or rose-tinted ending to any of these situations, but we *will* see how all four people can face up to their personal disaster – their own storm – and cope with it as best they can.

I'll keep to a minimum any explanation of psychological theories behind what we're talking about (there are references and further reading suggestions at the end of the book if you want to pursue them). On the chance that someone reading this may well be facing a major crisis, there's a benefit in keeping it concise. Even so, it's always worth trying to pull together the key points at the end of a chapter, just to reinforce the message.

## Key points

- Really bad things can happen, and you can't always stop them; you have to face the storm.
- Just because they happen, doesn't mean you're helpless.
- The keys to facing a disaster are
  - understanding what's happening to you
  - having coping strategies to make the best of a bad situation.
- Palliative care helps people to cope with fatal illness and bereavement, and some of the lessons learned there can help you to become more resilient to other sorts of crises.

# 2

# Gale warning

## Realising you're in trouble

### The day before the world changed

If you're reading this book because you're currently facing up to an imminent crisis, it might seem pointless to be thinking about what life was like before you found out about it. But (as with so many things), to make sense of where we are, we often need to take account of how we got here.

When we are struggling with a significant crisis, it can feel as if life before it came along was ideal, and now it's awful. That may of course be true. More often, though, the new problem occurs in the context of the complicated, messy and imperfect lives that most us live, most of the time. You can, however, end up 'idealising the past': looking back (in comparison to current difficulties) life looked easy and idyllic, even if in reality it felt far from that at the time. That's an understandable reaction, but it can be quite unhelpful:

- It makes the present seem even worse in comparison to the idealised past.
- If you're not going to be able to return to your life before the crisis, it becomes harder to reconcile yourself in the long term to the life you actually have (see Chapter 4).
- You may end up trying to solve the wrong problem (e.g. if marital strain to the verge of breakdown is seen as principally a consequence of a current financial crisis, then all effort may be put into the finances, allowing pre-existing marital problems to worsen irretrievably).

- Even if you manage to return to 'normal' after the crisis is over, life may feel unsatisfactory compared to the fantasy of the idealised life before it.

There are several aspects of pre-crisis life which play a part in coping with the crisis itself. These factors include the financial (e.g. do you have the money to afford a good lawyer?), the practical (have you got a permanent address and access to a telephone?), the physical (do you have the health and mobility to do whatever the crisis will require?) and the social (e.g. how close a social support network you have). A person's general psychological state will also matter; a new crisis confronting someone who is already depressed, stressed or suffering from 'burn-out' will be all the harder to face up to (although it's worth saying that people who have suffered a lifetime of anxiety about relatively minor things will sometimes astonish everyone by coping magnificently with a significant crisis).

But the big, dramatic emotional states (like depression) are not the main way in which psychological factors will influence how bad news is received, understood and acted upon. Our response to a crisis (or, indeed, any situation) is crucially determined by the beliefs and understanding of the world that we have been forming throughout our lives so far. These could be quite concrete beliefs like 'I'm fit enough to climb up steps whenever I want to'. Or they could be rules for living by, such as 'Marriage is for life – if you work hard enough at a relationship it will last'. Alternatively they might be far more abstract principles like 'By and large, people get what they deserve in this life'.

Consider the effects that holding a basic belief of 'I'm unlucky; I always get the worst possible outcome of things' might have on how you receive bad news, and the decisions you base on it. When some expert (e.g. your doctor or your lawyer) sets out a range of possible outcomes to your current situation, if you assume the very worst will come true, you may end up making decisions which would be appropriate for that specific (worst) outcome, but which are unhelpful for all the others.

Helen vividly remembers her father being diagnosed with bowel cancer a few years ago. His must have been detected at an earlier stage than hers, as there were more treatment options open to him. His consultant offered him a course of chemotherapy, explaining that it could have several outcomes: there was a chance that it could bring long-term remission of the cancer, more probably it would delay the cancer from advancing for a couple of years, but there was also a small possibility it would have no effect and the cancer would progress rapidly despite the treatment. A lifelong pessimist, Helen's father tended to believe that 'For me, anything that *can* go badly, *will* go badly'. So he assumed that the treatment was bound to be ineffective for him, so why bother putting himself through the effort and side-effects when it was pointless anyway? He decided to opt out of a treatment which could have been helpful.

Helen promised herself that she'd never take that approach, and would try anything that was offered.

---

**Try this now:**

Think of a situation you have been faced with where a range of outcomes was possible. Try to come up with the most optimistic and the most pessimistic expectations that a person might hold about it, and identify the consequences of holding each. Now spell out a more neutral approach and say how that would be different.

If, once you've finished this task (or any of the others in this book), you're feeling more worried or down, take a few minutes' break to do something neutral (make a cup of tea, get a breath of fresh air). And then read on, because this book is about the positive things we can do in the face of problems, even if thinking about them feels uncomfortable.

---

Some people seem purposefully to adopt a strategy we call 'protective pessimism';[3] by expecting the worst, they seek to avoid disappointment if things do go badly, but will be pleasantly surprised if things go even averagely well. Many of us do this to an extent, and it can be very effective in cushioning against disappointment, particularly where we're not talking about very significant risks. However, as with more global pessimism, we must beware that it doesn't sap hope and make us too resigned and passive; that way can easily lead to the 'self-fulfilling prophecy', where expectation of failure leads to reduced effort, making failure inevitable.

We've looked at how pre-existing pessimistic beliefs may influence how bad news is received, interpreted and acted upon. It's not hard to see how other underlying assumptions might also play out: 'If you want a job doing, do it yourself', 'Never trust a doctor/lawyer/plumber/etc.', 'Why should anyone care about me?' These beliefs (and the millions of others that humans are capable of holding) end up being key determinants of how people react to situations, by shaping how they interpret them. Indeed, it seems that one of the basic rules of human psychology is this:

People are not moved by events, but by the view they take of them.

This idea has a long history: it was coined nearly 2000 years ago by the philosopher Epictetus (being a disabled Roman slave before becoming a famous Stoic philosopher, he probably knew a thing or two about suffering).[4] It's become a foundation of one of the dominant models of applied psychology (cognitive behavioural therapy), where learning to identify and challenge inaccurate and unhelpful thoughts is used to help a person cope with a variety of emotional and behavioural problems.

We've got to be a little careful here, though. While it's sometimes possible, having identified these negative thoughts and beliefs, to challenge them and learn to replace them with something more helpful, that's not always the case. Sometimes, the more we get into an argument with the thoughts that pop up, the more we become tangled up with them, and we end up going over and over the same territory even more. So our attempts to defeat these unhelpful thoughts actually wind up with them being on our minds even more.

If that happens, it can be better not to bother answering back against those troubling thoughts, but rather recognise them for what they truly are – thoughts, fleeting words and pictures created by your mind which may or may not be accurate, but at this moment are just thoughts. And if they show up often, then name them:

'Oh, here's my "I'll never cope" thought.'

Simple as it sounds, learning to 'distance' yourself from the thought rather than getting tangled up with what it says to you can be a very effective way to reduce its power over you. It's a technique called 'defusion'.

---

**Try this defusion technique:**

- Make a list of three troubling, unhelpful or self-critical thoughts that you're prone to.
- Rehearse each one to yourself ten times, always starting with 'This is my thought that . . .'
- Write each one on a piece of card and carry it around with you.
- Next time the thought pops up by itself, repeat it to yourself saying 'Oh, here's my thought that. . .', get out the card with the thought written on it, and take a good look.

It might sound as if that would make you have the thought more often; actually it gets you used to 'stepping back' from the thought when it occurs.

---

### Realising there's a problem

Many of us will be able to recall those gut-dropping moments when you realise that something has gone horribly wrong. A school friend of mine once wrote what he thought was an excellent exam essay on the 'Causes of the First World War'; I can still remember his expression afterwards when he realised the question had actually asked for the '*Consequences* of the First World War'. In learning that he had misread a single word, I think he suddenly had visions of dropped grades, failing to get into the university he wanted, not getting into his career of choice, and so on and so on. Mind you, the last I heard he was a successful barrister, so it clearly didn't do too much damage in the long term.

With major crises, it may equally be that there is a distinct moment when you move from thinking that things are broadly OK, and life is going along quite normally, to realising that there is serious trouble looming.

Generally, though, that process is a more gradual one. Think of watching your team lose a crucial cup match. You start optimistic of getting a solid victory and a place in the next round. Early on, even though your team doesn't score, and the opposition get a goal before half-time, there's still plenty of time for a comeback. As the second half progresses and the opposition score again, the game is still winnable, but the need to get on and score gets more and more pressing as time passes. A draw starts to look attractive, and maybe the best that can now be achieved. As the minutes tick by, even a draw begins to look unlikely. The game isn't officially lost until the final whistle blows, but the inevitability of the result (and its consequences) has gradually sunk in before then; there is no single moment of transition from 'not knowing' to 'knowing' that the game is lost.

That's a gradual process, even if it takes place over a few (agonising) minutes. Many crises in life become gradually apparent only over weeks, months or years. For example, temporary conflicts and differences between a couple get less temporary, worsen rather than improve until it becomes clear that a happy life together just isn't going to happen.

Peter knew that, as a start-up company, his new venture could expect a tough first year establishing itself. Each new order gave him some hope that word was spreading, and that success might begin to snowball. So, even though he had to go further into debt to tide the company over, he mostly felt confident that he was about to turn a corner. When he first saw adverts from bigger rivals offering the same service as his (only cheaper), he knew the struggle would be greater, but planned to change his marketing approach. Then his suppliers raised the price of raw materials, and he had higher equipment maintenance bills than he expected. Gradually, it became apparent that the business was simply not going to thrive, and could only limp along until the banks started to call in their loans. Still, though, Peter fantasised about the unexpected huge order that could turn everything around.

And that, of course, is just looking at the crises that do come to pass. We are also used to there being many potential disasters which never develop, or are solved before they become a problem. So, a cough could potentially end up being the first sign of lung cancer, but it is hugely more likely to turn out to be just a cough.

Equally, in business, a balance sheet that doesn't add up might be the first inkling that you're the victim of a massive fraud, but is probably because you've forgotten to copy a column of figures across from the previous page. It's often only after the event that you can see what were the first signs of the problems to come. With the benefit of hindsight, we can end up feeling stupid or angry at ourselves for having missed them, or indeed angry at others (partner, accountant, doctor) for not seeing them in time to take corrective action.

We come across this situation a lot in cancer treatment and palliative care. Sadly, it's true that symptoms are sometimes missed which shouldn't have been, and in some cases that makes a difference to how treatable and/or survivable the disease is (and sometimes it doesn't). Many times, though, there's no way of knowing that a general symptom like backache, tiredness, irritability or a cough are going to be anything more than they appear to be. In this example, as in non-medical equivalents, a great deal of emotional and practical effort can end up being focused on the perceived culprit for the problem, which might be better spent on dealing with the problem itself. So, while we should always try to reflect on what's happened to learn from it, beware the dangers of 'hindsighting'![5]

What about those cases where the bad news isn't discovered (rapidly or gradually) by the individual in question, but has to be imparted? There are many professions where this is routinely part of the job, from 'It'll need a new radiator system', through 'Your application has not been successful' to 'We couldn't remove all of the tumour'. It's probably fair to say that professions vary in how much care they take over communicating bad news; it's certainly a huge consideration in healthcare these days, though sadly we're very far from doing it well all the time. These shortfalls will sometimes be due to poor training, lack of aptitude, or other pressures getting in the way. But what people don't always realise is that there is no single 'right way' to do it, in the sense that what would be a perfect approach and wording in explaining to one person might be disastrous to another.

Helen has made friends with Zoë, a young woman with a different cancer, but who attends for chemotherapy at the same time as her. They spend some of the seemingly endless time in the waiting room comparing notes on the staff they see. Zoë says that, although she trusts their consultant Dr Vickery, she gets irritated by him 'beating around the bush' – he's so busy asking what she thinks and feels that she just wants him to get on with it and tell her what's happening, and what she should do. She actually prefers the assistant they sometimes see, Dr Hewin, who gives her information straight, as one adult to another. Helen's a bit taken aback by this; she thinks Dr Hewin's too brutal and unsympathetic; Dr Vickery seems much more interested, concerned and humane. Rather than fall out about their differences, the conversation moves onto whispered, giggling speculation about how the two doctors' different styles might be reflected in their performance in bed . . .

It's always worth remembering that amid the serious business of dealing with serious events, human nature and the need for humour will still prevail at times.

This isn't the place for going into detail about how we teach doctors, nurses and other healthcare staff how to deal with the differing needs of their patients. By checking out what the person already knows, though, and staying tuned in to how they're reacting, one can usually get the necessary information across in the least damaging way possible.[6] And that's the point – while it's vital that we don't (through poor communication) make a bad situation even worse, even the best communication skills in the world can't make it feel OK to hear catastrophically bad news.

So much for the challenge facing the person breaking the bad news; what can *you*, as the person receiving it, do? It might seem that all you can do is sit and listen, but that's not so. Dependent upon the precise context (e.g. talking to a garage mechanic versus a consultant surgeon, whether or not you have a suspicion that you might be about to receive bad news) you can do some or all of the following.

- Consider taking someone along with you – the benefits can be emotional support and another pair of ears for you to compare your memory of the conversation with afterwards. For some, the downside can be feeling the pressure of 'keeping up appearances' in front of your partner or friend, or feeling inhibited from asking certain questions in case *they* disapprove or aren't ready to hear it.
- Think about questions in advance that you think you'll want answering and *write them down*, then have the piece of paper and a pen in your hand as you sit down ready to take notes. Otherwise, there's a very strong chance you'll be so absorbed in what you are being told that you'll forget your questions (or the answers).
- Ask for clarification. Don't worry about asking for words or phrases to be explained or repeated; above

all, try not to worry about seeming stupid. It's more foolish to nod and go along with something knowing that you don't understand it, because ultimately it's *you* that this catastrophe is happening to, not normally the person who's telling you about it.

- Ask if you can have a written summary, whether that's just a few key terms written down there and then, or a fuller letter to be sent (or copied) to you afterwards.

- Check back your understanding at the end of being told – you may think you've grasped it, but you might have got the wrong idea. Try 'So let me see if I've got this straight; you're saying that . . .'

- Make sure you're clear about what happens next; are there recommendations for what you should be doing (which, of course, you can decide whether to follow or not), or is the other person taking responsibility for whatever action is needed?

- You may want to ask further questions, or get more information later on (perhaps once the initial news has 'sunk in'). Find out how you'll best get access to it.

- Straight afterwards, write down a brief account for yourself to keep, with details of what was said, who was present, and future steps to be taken.

Being able to do some of the above should reduce the chance that, five minutes after you've left the person, you'll be thinking 'What went on there?' However, it is only reducing the chance, not eliminating it; you mustn't expect yourself to be as calm, rational and focused as you usually are. There are lots of reasons for this: news can take a person by surprise, leave them feeling 'in shock', or emotionally overwhelmed, or – and this is quite common – one part of the news (maybe a single word like 'cancer', 'prison' or 'divorce') may be latched onto, and drown out everything else that's said.[7]

Debbie first heard about the factory closure on the local TV news; she'd been aware that there'd been gossip about job losses around the factory floor for the previous few days, but made a point of never paying attention to that sort of thing – there was always something going round, and it usually turned out to be wrong. When she saw a picture of her workplace on the TV screen, she listened in, but afterwards could only remember the words 'the Harker Textile mill at Dunmouth is set to close with the loss of all 800 jobs'. She had no recollection of any of the other information about why the decision had been made, when it might happen, or the reaction of the local MP.

There are endless ways in which people react to bad news; the sequence often spoken about (partly following the work of a famous writer and activist Elisabeth Kübler-Ross)[8] of denial – fear/anger – depression – acceptance is so far from universal that it's probably not a good idea to expect those particular things in that particular sequence; we'll look at this in more detail in Chapters 4 and 10. Emotionally, pretty well anything goes early on in a crisis, and the same person will even react differently on different occasions. It is better, then, not to expect any reaction in particular, but to try to deal with whatever arises; that's something we'll address in some depth in Chapter 10.

But once it becomes clear that a crisis really is looming, what do you do then? That's what most of the rest of this book is about – how you 'get your head around it' and what you do to try to cope as well as you can.

## Key points

- Beware of looking back on life before the crisis as perfect; a distorted view of the past can make the present and the future even harder to deal with.
- Be aware of the existing factors that provide some of the raw materials for coping:
  - your practical circumstances
  - your financial state

- - your physical health
  - your social situation
  - your psychological state (mood, disposition, and outlook).
- How people react to events depends (largely) on the view they take of them.
- Extremes of pessimism or optimism carry a high price.
- Disasters often become apparent gradually – and they may be impossible to spot at first.
- Don't waste energy blaming yourself or others for not spotting something that was only obvious with hindsight.
- Bad news is still bad news even if it's broken to you well.
- Don't just *receive* bad news; take an active part in meetings or consultations where bad news may be given (see suggestions above).

# 3

# Listening to the forecasts
## Making sense of it

### Why bother?

As should be clear by now, being able to make sense of the situation you find yourself in is one of the cornerstones of coping with crises. Some people would argue that this need to understand what's going on, rather than just react to the situation in front of us, is one of the defining characteristics of humans. Of course, you see elements of it in other species (witness a chimp investigating a child's activity centre), but it seems to be we humans who take it to the extreme. Why do we bother? Making sense of the world – be that following the news, reading up on a specific topic, trying to work out how a conjurer performed a trick – rarely makes much immediate difference to whether we survive, have enough to eat, or remain safe. Yet maybe there's so much advantage in figuring out how our immediate environment works ('Where do the tigers get into the valley from?' 'How can we make the food grow *here*, rather than having to go looking for it?') that we evolved brains that are good at it, and everything else comes along because of it.[9]

Some would argue that this ability to look and think ahead is one of our great strengths, and comes at a great cost; because we can imagine and think about things that aren't in front of us, we can solve problems that haven't happened yet, but we can also be tortured by worries that aren't real.[10] So knowing and thinking ahead has costs as well as benefits.

Yes, there are limits to what we might feel compelled to understand (let's face it, most of us can live a happy enough life without understanding quantum theory), and we'll see below that people differ in their compulsion to find out about things. By and large, though, we can argue that there's a basic human drive to make sense of things, not usually as strong as the drive to get oxygen, water or food, but still important enough that we feel uncomfortable if we can't make sense of something that seems important to us.

By the way, I'm tending to use the phrase 'making sense' here; people might instead say 'understand'. There are two reasons why I'm not: first, 'understanding' in the sense of *comprehending* can easily get confused with 'understanding' meaning *feel compassion or empathy for*, or even *forgive*. This can be an unfortunate confusion, if you imagine someone saying 'After watching that documentary, I can understand why Hitler invaded Poland'. Second, 'understanding' what is happening can imply that there is a single *true* version of events, and that you've 'got it'. In reality, there can be many ways of looking at a situation, and many different conclusions that can be reached. In particular, this understanding may be something you build for yourself, differently from how anyone else would see it; so, you would be literally *making* sense of the situation.

When Anil first learned about Sarah's affair at work, he couldn't understand why it had happened; their relationship seemed a good one, and there had been no more arguments than usual recently. Sarah herself, though tearfully apologetic, and adamant that it would never happen again, couldn't explain why she had done it; she just described it as a 'stupid mistake' and begged Anil not to go over and over it, but work together to rebuild their relationship. Although he didn't want to jeopardise their relationship further by more questioning, Anil spent a lot of time thinking about 'why'. He gradually came to the conclusion that Sarah had panicked a little at their relationship settling down even further and moving towards parenthood, which he was sure scared her. Surely, then,

> this affair was some last, impulsive act of rebellion before committing to being a lifelong partner and mother?

As this example shows us, how we make sense of things can be influenced by many things, including what we really *want* to be true.

It's also important not to confuse this with 'finding a meaning'. That's talking about finding some underlying message, significance, purpose or philosophical insight in your experience. Examples might include 'This has shown me I'm a strong person', 'This was sent as a test from God' or 'This has allowed me to appreciate life for the first time'.

> At first, Debbie felt disappointed and angry that all her efforts to build a decent life for herself and her daughter would soon be undone, and even needed to turn to her pastor to ask him why God would do this to her. On his encouragement, she spent time reflecting and praying. She came to the conclusion that, just as she had faced teenage pregnancy, single motherhood, poverty and the temptations of drink and drugs, yet come through stronger and a better person, then maybe this was one more adversity to face in order to show her daughter (and others on the estate) that there is always hope.
>
> In her darker moments, though, she occasionally wonders if she is being punished for taking too much pride in her achievements.

If you do find a meaning, that may be both important and helpful for you; however, many people cannot find some higher significance, or come to the conclusion that there is none to be found. That does not mean that they cope less well.

This is not simply an abstract argument about the definitions of words. If you can bear in mind that making sense of something doesn't mean you have to like it, forgive it or gain from it, or that anyone else agrees with you about it, then you'll be more able to think clearly in difficult situations which others are struggling to deal with.[11]

One morning, on the way to chemotherapy, Helen's friend Zoë asks her, 'Do you ever think about the cancer, and ask "Why me?"' Helen pauses for a few moments, and says, 'I used to, and then one day I thought "Well, why *not* me?", and the question doesn't seem to bother me any more.'

## What sort of information you need

When you do 'make sense', you're forming a *mental representation*, a kind of explanation or model (some would say 'story') of the thing in your own head. That's what happens (let's hope) if someone explains how to get somewhere, or how to use a computer program: you listen, form a representation in your head of the things being discussed, and then (again, let's hope) make use of it as you follow the route, or try to use the program.

Exactly what information you need to form a useful representation of something will depend on several things. These include:

- what kind of situation or thing is being described (e.g. a movie, a motor car, a skill, a threat)
- what you already know or think about it (however accurate or not that is)
- what kind of person you are
- what information is or isn't available anyway.

Let's take those in turn.

### *What kind of situation*

Different situations require different information; some might be a list of rules (e.g. rules of a sport), for others a list of information (train and bus times for a complex journey), and frequently a mixture of both. For some situations, we know what kinds of information people tend to seek. The best-researched example is probably health, where we know the most commonly sought information about a disease you've just been diagnosed with are 'What's it like? What'll it do to me? How did I get it? Is it going to get better, stay like this or get worse? Is there anything that can done to cure or control it?' (Not for nothing is this called the 'common sense model of illness'!)[12]

We don't know as much about reactions to other kinds of problem, though some people would argue that for most new situations if you try to find out Who, What, Where, Why, When and How, you'll be making a good start (the poet Kipling referred to these words as his 'six honest serving men – they taught me all I knew').[13]

A few years ago, before his current business difficulties, Peter started helping to run the local scout troop. One evening, he heard a rumour that the local council was going to close down and then sell the community centre that the scout troop used. Before deciding how to proceed, he tried to find out:

- **Who** was suggesting this plan
- **What** had actually been said
- **Where** the idea had been discussed
- **Why** they were planning to close it
- **When** they were planning to close it
- **How** they were planning to go about it.

This information allowed him to brief all the other interested parties, and together work out how (and indeed whether) to campaign against the closure.

### *What you already know*

We hardly ever come to a situation without any previous knowledge or ideas on the subject. We may have direct experience, or good information from other people, or (more frequently for new situations) some mishmash of assumptions, prejudices, analogies from other situations that strike us as similar, and things we've seen on TV. Think about that last point for a moment: most of us are lucky enough never to have experienced a hostage situation, serious earthquake or alien invasion, yet years of TV and movie watching have given us detailed representations of what 'always' happens. The same may well be true of more frequent disasters like redundancy, divorce, imprisonment or terminal illness.

This is another great 'trick' that humans have developed: in entirely novel situations, we don't freeze because we know nothing about them; instead, we apply the nearest set of beliefs and experiences (however we gained them) that we already have, and gradually adjust it to meet the new situation.

> Peter has never been to prison; if he does end up going there, the number of things to learn to help him survive this unfamiliar and threatening environment will be daunting. He did, however, spend a few years in the army when younger, and might be able to apply many of the same 'rules' for dealing with authority, avoiding becoming marked out as a victim, and coping with confinement and boredom.

So the new information we seek and/or receive is actually being slotted into a pre-existing mental representation, which is itself being gradually adjusted[14] (more on that later).

This process is not without drawbacks, however, as assumptions based on other experiences may be inaccurate and/or unhelpful.

> One of the reasons that Helen never suspected that her digestive problems might be cancer was that her father was diagnosed with – and ultimately died of – bowel cancer some years earlier. He started to lose weight, and then found he was passing blood, which rapidly led to his being taken in for tests, and receiving his diagnosis. Because Helen hadn't lost any weight or passed blood (and she certainly checked), she reasoned that whatever was causing her stomach discomfort and cycles of constipation and diarrhoea, it couldn't be cancer, because she knew how *that* presents.

So, it's important when facing new and significant situations not to rely too much on what we think we already know. The famous Stoic philosopher Marcus Aurelius warned us always to pay attention to what a thing really is at heart,[15] not what we assume it is (and Hannibal Lecter quoted that advice in *The Silence of the Lambs*, so it must be true!). When young doctors are taught these days how to interview patients, or indeed to break bad news, they're always encouraged to start off by finding out what the patient already knows. Despite the occasional fear that this will lead to an unmanageably long consultation (not true, actually; the resultant conversation is usually the same length or shorter, but is better 'targeted', so has a better outcome),[16] this allows any unhelpful misunderstandings to be dealt with before they can interfere with the new information you're about to be given.

---

**Try this now:**

You can effectively do the same for yourself; when facing your crisis, try to find time to sit down and write out a list of everything you know about the situation and what is likely to happen. Then go back thorough your list and pick out:

- those things that you definitely know for certain
- what you probably know, but might benefit from double-checking
- things that are guesses (which might still turn out to be right – sometimes our guesses are less blind than we assume), or assumptions for which we can find no evidence other than TV or films.

---

No two people would come up with identical lists, and that's not just due to differences in the information they already have.

### *What kind of person you are*

We actually differ in our preferences for information. In life generally, some people seem to be information addicts – watching the 24-hour news channels, always reading non-fiction. Others are far more selective, content just to know what they need to about what matters most to them.

If we start talking specifically about threatening situations, we see that distinction played out all the more clearly. Some individuals seem to be prone to seeking as much information as possible about the threat in question; they stay alert for any mention in the papers, read every booklet going and (these days) may spend a lot of time seeking relevant information on the internet. Referred to as 'monitors' in the research,[17] they will begin to feel more anxious if they cannot find answers to the questions they have in mind. In contrast, others, who are termed 'blunters', cope better by cutting down the amount of threat-related information they expose themselves to; this doesn't necessarily imply a complete 'head in the sand' attitude, but does often involve avoiding situations where they might see or hear more than they wanted to. So, in palliative care, someone with 'monitor' tendencies might look at the cancer information websites, attend support groups, turn up at clinic appointments with a carefully prepared list of questions for the consultant or specialist nurse, and take a keen interest in any blood test results or X-rays of tumour response to treatment. The 'blunter' approach might involve a request to the doctor to 'Tell me what I've got, tell me what treatment you recommend, but don't tell me any odds or how long you think I have left'.

Given the discussions above about the human drive to make sense of situations, it would be tempting to conclude that information-seeking ('monitoring') must be a good thing, and information-limiting ('blunting') is a bad thing. Actually, there are pros and cons to each.

The pros of seeking out all possible information include having the chance to be prepared for things that might happen, having plenty of opportunity – and more time – to sort out your priorities, and feeling more confident when dealing with others (including 'experts' such as doctors, lawyers or accountants) who become involved.

The cons of extensive information-seeking are that it can be very time-consuming – try an internet search on the word 'cancer' and you'll see what I mean. Not surprising, then, that information-seeking can make a person confused and exhausted from trying to find the right information – particularly that which applies to them. The information you find will not always be good news; it will not be specific to your exact situation, and it will often be uncertain. In effect you may read of 100 bad outcomes, 99 of which are not going to happen to you – though you won't know that until after the event. And some of that information will be just plain wrong.

In some people, the search for information can become an obsession; and, like many obsessional behaviours, the more one indulges in it, the greater the need to indulge it more.[18] This is especially true if you are seeking reassurance: if you find it, you may feel better for a while, but then the doubts will creep in, and you'll need to seek more reassurance, more quickly. In extreme cases, this can become like a drug habit, where you need to seek bigger and bigger 'fixes' of reassurance, more and more frequently, but which are never satisfying for long.

Peter has always managed his work by trying to stay fully informed; at his old job, he used to have a poster saying 'Knowledge is Power' above his desk. Now he's worried about the possibility of fraud charges, he is spending a lot of time reading about the law, searching the internet for records of similar cases, and what punishments were received. Indeed, sometimes he'll wake in the early hours, get up and go to the computer because he's thought of another aspect of his situation; if he then finds relevant positive information, he'll feel reassured for a while. But by the next morning, he's begun to doubt the credibility of what he's read, and he's back on the internet searching again.

An information-limiting (or 'blunter') strategy might save him some sleepless nights, but would also prevent the preparedness and thinking time discussed above. There may also be additional costs to avoiding sources of information; you may shun those who could help you, for fear of what you might hear. You may also distance yourself from friends or family for the same reasons.

Yet, such a strategy may actually allow you to carry on functioning in the face of disaster, when (for you) facing up to the facts may be so overwhelming as to be disabling.

> Debbie has always believed that there are simply too many things in the world that you could worry about if you chose to. She prefers to focus on what's immediately relevant and get on with things. So, when it comes to the job loss, she decides that she'll be told when an actual closure date is confirmed; until then, as there's not much she can do to change what happens to the factory, she'll just throw herself into her church and community activities instead.

As ever, it probably comes down to personal preference, that some approaches simply suit some people better. More worried about being unaware of a possible outcome than hearing about ones that don't happen? Fine – seek that information. Know that you'd find yourself worrying about a million things that end up not happening? By all means limit your information search – though it helps if you trust that there are others around (your partner, your nurse, your accountant, your lawyer) who are keeping their eye on the ball, just in case one of those pieces of information you're steering clear of turns out to be vital.

---

**Try this now:**

Think of a crisis you could face (or are facing) and try to work out all the different questions you could seek answers to – why it's happening, what its most predictable effects are, what the less likely outcomes might be, who else has experienced it, what resources might be out there for coping, and so on and so on. Now, just regarding that list of questions (and not seeking any answers to them): does the prospect of keeping on top of that information (accepting that much of it will be speculative, uncertain or just plain unavailable) seem like giving you a sense of control and coping? Or does it fill you with a sense of dread and panic? That may give you a pointer towards how to approach information-seeking in a crisis.

But, don't forget that we treat different pieces of information differently; I've known people want all the information available on treatment options for their condition, but have asked for (and as far as possible, we've provided them with) it without any mention of likely survival times.

### What information is or isn't available

A final twist to this concerns the type of information available. All of the above decisions about what information is desired, personal preferences and so on would be difficult enough if all the information were potentially available in an accessible, comprehensible and reliable manner. In truth, information about future negative events is likely to be uncertain, complex and not easily available.

#### Information from 'expert sources'

None of us can know everything, and it makes sense to approach people with relevant expertise when we want to know more. As well as individual experts (doctors, lawyers, accountants), sources can include books, newspaper articles or websites. The dilemma comes in knowing which expert source, and how far to trust the information you receive. Search the internet enough, and you will find 'information' saying pretty well anything, and offering solutions or cures for any problem imaginable. The trouble is that the information will often be contradictory and much of it wrong, and even potentially dangerous.

> As it becomes clear to Anil that his relationship with Sarah is in trouble, he decides to learn more about how relationships work. He avidly reads articles in women's magazines, watches TV programmes, and works his way along the 'Relationships' shelf at his local bookshop. The trouble is, every opinion seems to be coming from a different direction: he hears that relationship problems are about sexual politics, or they're about evolutionary differences between the sexes, or astrological incompatibility or unhelpful energy flows within the home due to the position of furniture. Although he's happy to be open-minded about any of these, Anil has the feeling that as he reads and watches more and more, he is becoming less and less clear about what to do.

In the face of this difficulty, some people try asking the same question of a series of 'expert' sources, looking for a consistent answer between those sources. The danger here is that, even if all expert sources actually agree (rare enough!), they will differ in their way of explaining it and the vocabulary used. Unfortunately, to the listener who is new to the topic these differences will seem like contradictions, undermining confidence and increasing confusion.

Beware also of the fact that we would all like certain things to be true – that there really is a miracle cure for your disease, that a management buyout will save the factory and so on; there is a danger that we choose to believe those sources that are saying what we want to hear.[19] So, we ignore a hundred reputable voices saying that sensible eating and exercise are the answer to obesity, and choose to believe instead the quack offering the latest ten-day fad diet.

Sometimes, the issue is that the (genuine) expert won't answer the most important question; in palliative care, that may be 'How long do I have left?', or in a law case it could be 'How much will the settlement be?' It's difficult to know what to make of that, and people may come to different conclusions about *why* the expert is not answering:

- Perhaps they don't know, but someone more competent would.
- Perhaps they don't know because no one can possibly know.
- Perhaps they do know, but are withholding the information for some reason.

It might be important to work out which is the case, but how tactfully you want to challenge your 'expert' is up to you!

### Information from 'personal experience'

It's understandable that we put a lot of weight on the experiences of others who have 'been there' and personally faced up to the problem in question. We can certainly gain new insights, ideas and strategies from them, and often a sense of solidarity, countering the sensation that we are all alone with our problem. These are some of the main benefits of support groups for people with a particular problem.

What you can't necessarily get from this source, though, is information specific to your own particular situation (which, after all, is the only one that really matters to you), simply because that situation is, in fine detail, unique. Obvious as that may sound, people forget that fact every day. Because one person has direct, personal experience of, say, prostate cancer absolutely does not mean that they truly 'know what you are going through' when you have it. They may well have some points in common with you, but the detail of their disease, bodily response, treatment package, side-effects, personality, history, social setting and so on will be different, and so their experience, their reactions and their outcomes will be different too. Their support, advice and experience might well prove helpful, but it mustn't be mistaken for hard predictive information.

Anil tries not to discuss his problems at work, but ends up admitting his difficulties to a colleague, Barry, while away at a conference. It turns out that Barry's relationship also broke down in the last year. Although he is initially keen to swap experiences with someone else, and wants to hear advice on how to handle his problems, Anil gradually realises that Barry's relationship problems were very different from his own, and his advice to 'Insist she changes, or walk out on her' just doesn't seem right for Anil.

So, as previously noted, it can be a valuable experience to look at the information that (you think) you already have, and consider how confident you are in its source, and think what else you might want to seek and where you might get it.

We can see, then, that there are many things shaping the information a person has about their situation, and how they deal with it. But it gets even more complicated when we look at that person in the context of others – professionals, friends and family members, because then it's not just a question of one person's preferences and actions – others will have to make decisions about what information they need to discuss.

For instance, an individual choosing to avoid discussing matters with their doctor/lawyer/accountant can create dilemmas for the professional. What if someone asked you not to tell them something, and they are making a decision you think they will come to regret on the basis of their incomplete knowledge? What if you suspect they would want to know more if they realised what the truth was? When is it right to discuss a possible outcome which is very, very unlikely to happen, but would be terrible if it did? There are good reasons why 'Ethics' is one of the teaching blocks in most palliative care courses.

The problem is, these aren't just ethical dilemmas for those who are paid to deal with them, as (dependent on the problem in question) different members of your family, practice or work group may face the same dilemmas. They too may find themselves in possession of levels of information at odds with your own preferences. And this comes down to the differences between participants in the same situation in terms of their need for, preferences about, and access to, relevant information.

Those family members or colleagues really are 'players' in a crisis. It may be your cancer, or your court case, but it is almost certainly going to alter the lives of people around you, so they (in turn) will need to make sense of it for themselves, in order to cope as best they can. Their information needs may well be different, though, because of the different role they are playing in the crisis, their own preferences, or characteristics. A good example here is age: sometimes, people make assumptions that the very young and the very old shouldn't be told too much about a crisis in the family. Yet in both cases, people generally spot that *something* is going on, and if denied all access to information, their 'making sense' will have little to go on, leaving them either puzzled or making up something inaccurate and possibly worse than reality.[20]

> Peter's son is in his second year at university and only gets home every few months. Against his wife's better judgement, Peter decides that their son shouldn't be told yet about the bankruptcy and legal threats; he reasons that the stress of knowing would harm his studies. As nothing is yet certain, better to delay telling him as long as possible.
>
> This strategy works for the weekly phone call home during term-time. However, when he comes to stay over Easter, he soon picks up the feeling that there is a lot of tension about, and something that he is not being told; intense, whispered conversations end abruptly when he walks into the room. He comes to the conclusion that his parents' relationship is in trouble; he's heard of other couples splitting up once their children have left home – he becomes convinced that this is about to happen to his parents.

So, we see that attempting to 'make sense' of an important situation is as close to a universal human instinct as any. However, how we achieve that 'sense' (and how *far* we achieve it) will vary hugely depending on the nature of the situation, our own personalities and the kinds of information available to us. And it's unlikely to be a one-off process; as the crisis develops, situations will change, mental representations will need updating or revising and new information will need to be sought, or dealt with.

It's one thing to make sense of a situation, but something rather different to 'get used to it'. And that's what we need to consider next.

## Key points

- The urge to make sense of a situation is a basic human drive.
- When we're in a new situation, we often fall back on what we know about other situations that seem similar, but that can lead us into mistakes if we're not careful; so check what you actually know, and what you're just assuming.
- Be aware of your sources of information – don't trust a source just because you want to believe what they're saying.
- People differ in how much information they want, and everyone has a different balance point between too much and too little; work out what suits you.
- In the absence of information, people will come to their own conclusions – so be careful of trying to hide everything from children and elderly people.

# 4

# I can't believe it's going to hit us

## Getting used to it

### Going through the stages

Several years ago, I had a patient who was attempting to put his life back together after a whole series of disasters had befallen him – only some of which were self-inflicted. John was at times scathing about the abilities of professionals (myself included, I suspect) to understand what was going on for someone like him. So I told him I was shortly to give a lecture about adjusting to serious illness, and wondered what advice he'd want to offer the assembled surgeons, nurses, social workers and so on. He held my gaze for a while, then said:

'Tell them, you've got to just ****ing-well get over it.'

John's model of adjustment (with his permission, and properly attributed) remains a part of my lecture on adjustment to this day, and always goes down well. It certainly captures the avoidance of self-pity and the determination that you see in many people successfully coping with adversity.

The reason why the lecture doesn't end with John's statement is that it still leaves the question of *how* you 'get over it', and indeed whether we are ever genuinely 'over' events of this magnitude.

Probably the most famous theory of adjustment was originally applied to people getting used to the idea of dying, though it has been since applied to lots of other sudden adverse events. This is the model put forward by

Dr Elisabeth Kübler-Ross,[21] and suggests that people tend to go through several distinct phases in their reactions to bad news:

1 *Denial*: the initial tendency to disbelieve that the event is happening.
2 *Anger or anxiety*: feeling acutely stressed by it.
3 *Bargaining*: seeking any possible way out of the situation, even when deep down you know that is impossible.
4 *Despair*: speaks for itself really – feeling down, sad and helpless about the event.
5 *Acceptance*: finally feeling that you've come to terms with it, are neither stressed nor depressed by it, and can carry on.

This view has gained widespread acceptance, even to the point of appearing in an episode of *The Simpsons* – the ultimate marker of cultural acceptance.

Dr Kübler-Ross wasn't just dreaming this stuff up – she was basing her ideas on interviews with many people in exactly that situation. A parallel model of how people react to bereavement (by Professor Colin Murray Parkes) was based on his careful interviews with many widows.[22] And it isn't hard to see examples of all of those stages in people facing their own death, or reacting to the death of someone they love:

• Someone reacting with utter calm to news of their terminal illness, trying to carry on as before without making any changes or preparations.
• The man reacting with anger against the doctors, other family members, God and even his own wife for her death.

And the same things can apply to the other crises we're considering here:

Everyone who knows Debbie well sees the change in her the first few weeks after the factory closed. Although she goes through the motions of many of her usual responsibilities, she doesn't appear to be concentrating properly, seems distant and easily drifts off into a vacant state. The pastor of her church recognises this as a state of 'shock and numbness', part of a grief response to the loss of her work and the things that went with it. He advises Debbie's friends to treat her with patience, as it will surely pass.

It's true that people grieve for many things other than a death; like Debbie it can be the loss of a job, it can be for physical health, a happy phase of life or anything that has been a stable, familiar part of our lives.

Before we go much further, it's important to put in a caution about these models, or rather about how these models are often understood. For, although the authors point out that many variations can occur, at heart these models describe reactions as a series of stages – first this happens, then that, later that and finally . . . In reality, people can skip stages, go back to a previous one, experience something that's not in the model at all, and many will never reach acceptance, 'letting go' or 'moving on' as specified. I'd want to stress again that Kübler-Ross and Parkes were clear that such things also happened. But people often don't remember that kind of qualification, or they haven't read the original version, so they're expecting something different. And sometimes, when people's real reactions don't fit the (misunderstood) model, then the grieving person is seen as being peculiar or pathological. I've certainly had referrals for bereaved people 'because they have not cried yet'.

Such is the prevalence of the Kübler-Ross model that it was worth looking at specifically. But rather than look at all the other theories of responses to serious illness and death, perhaps we should focus on three core areas that crop up time and again in terms of the after-effects of bad events: adjustment, acceptance and denial.

**Adjustment**

We make adjustments all the time: we adjust the volume on our TV because someone's using a lawn-mower outside the window; someone might adjust an item of clothing because it doesn't fit any more. These are things that we alter because we're trying to compensate for a change in circumstances (i.e. the room has become too noisy to hear the TV, we have become too fat to fit into a pair of trousers). So, when we talk about adjusting to a change in our lives, what is it that we are really trying to alter? I supervised a bright trainee health psychologist who did a good piece of research on this: she interviewed in great depth a group of palliative care nurses (Macmillan nurses) about their experiences of supporting many thousands of terminally ill people through their adjustment to this devastating change in their lives. The analysis of their views showed that, in their experience, successful adjustment involved lots of changes, to what people did, to how they were with others, to their spiritual and religious beliefs, and to how they viewed themselves, and their future.[23]

Now, the changes in what they did – the behavioural changes – are going to be entirely dependent on the precise nature of the change in life, and the circumstances they live in. It could be as simple as sitting rather than standing while preparing food, or it could be a bigger challenge such as beginning to use a wheelchair in public.

A spiritual change might be an attempt to make sense of why such a thing should happen to you, while there are so many bad people in the world (remember in Chapter 3, Debbie came to the conclusion that her ill-fortune might be a test, or a punishment for pride). Again, though, it should be stressed that this is very far from a universal process; most people don't spend much time thinking about 'why me?'.

Of most interest to us here is how people's mental attitude to their situation alters, because, as we have already seen, the view we take of a situation is one of the main things that shapes our reactions to it.

One thing that adjustment is *not* is putting everything back to normal, making it just like before. Because, for the types of crises we're looking at in this book, the reality is that life will never be exactly the same again; some things are likely to be worse, there may just be one or two things that are better, but there are certainly going to be things that are different. The crucial thing here is not to strive for making everything the same as it was before – you'll probably fail, you'll be constantly comparing how things are now to how they were, and you may end up causing new problems by going after that impossible aim.

> As Helen starts to develop more symptoms, she tries her best not to let her illness disrupt family life. She carries on doing the school run, the shopping and taking Liam to swimming lessons and football club. Increasingly, though, these take so much out of her that she isn't capable of doing anything else. She feels guilty for failing at the things that would normally seem so easy to manage, and fears that she's letting down her family. It comes to a head on a day when she takes Liam to school, does the washing when she comes back, then tries to do the shopping. Not only does she have to give up halfway through, but on getting home she needs to lie down to recover and sleeps through school finishing time; she wakes to a concerned call from Liam's teacher wondering why he hasn't been picked up. Once she recovers from the surprise and the guilt and has calmed her distraught son down, she realises she's going to have to change her approach.

The real goal of adjustment is to deal with the new reality, to find an approach to life that fits how things actually are now, rather than how they used to be, or how you'd like them to be. We could say that adjustment is beginning to live your life according to a new reality. And that's going to require different strategies.

I often use the analogy from card games:

> You play the hand you've got now, not the one you had in the last game.

Whether you have a hand of cards that's all twos and threes, or all queens and kings, you'll play them a certain way to get the best result you can; but (crucially) how you play when you get the twos and threes will need to be different from how you did when you had queens and kings.

If you go as aggressively with a weaker hand, you'll lose more than if you base your play on the weaker cards you actually have; it's going to take a different approach to limit your losses now. This may sound obvious, but we all have a tendency, when faced with problems, to use strategies that have worked for us before.[24] Usually that makes good sense, but sometimes it's disastrous.

So take a person who's always succeeded by working harder, never giving in to tiredness, pain or illness. That may help with a lot of problems; but if the person has a serious back injury, then pushing themselves harder and harder when pain builds up is likely to make matters a whole lot worse. Yet learning to make that kind of change in approach can be really difficult. Why?

There are many kinds of explanation for that difficulty, but we're going to focus on one sort of explanation (a cognitive one, for those who are interested).

As we discussed in Chapter 3, we can talk about the whole set of knowledge, beliefs, ideas and assumptions about the world as mental *representations*. One of these representations is 'who I am'. That's not simply my name, but will also include what I believe to be my abilities, interests, physical characteristics, relationships and so on. So one part of that representation is that I can climb a flight of stairs fairly rapidly – which might be important if I need to get to the toilet in a hurry. Many of our judgements about how to react to the world (e.g. how long it takes me to get to the toilet) are based on underlying mental representations like these.[25] So if reality changes, those representations aren't accurate any more, and so our thoughts and actions based on them may well be inappropriate. If I get a back injury so that I can move only slowly, then even if I'm fully aware of the change, unless I 'update' that mental representation of myself properly, I might not leave enough time for getting to the toilet. But mental representations can be slow to change, and there may be a delay before they accurately reflect reality. The longer lasting, and more highly valued (or fundamental) that representation has been, the slower and/or more painful it may be to change.

It's probably not simply a case of an older, more inaccurate belief being erased and replaced by a more accurate new one. From what we know of how brains seem to work generally, it's more likely that the old and new versions exist side by side, but the more accurate one gradually becomes more dominant in shaping our reactions. The fact that, however weakened, the old version is still there may mean that under certain circumstances it becomes more active and has more of a say in our decisions and actions. For example, if I replace my car, and the indicator stalk is on the other side of the wheel from the one on the car I've been driving for a few years, it may take a little while for me to get used to that, even though I realise from the first time I drive that it's in a different position. Which is to say that the representation of the new stalk position gradually takes over from the representation that applied to the old car; but those old beliefs are still quietly there, so that if I'm rushed or stressed old habits can come back: rather than flashing my lights at someone, I might angrily wash my windscreen at them.

So, although it may be a slow and stressful business, with occasional slips back to previous assumptions, psychological adjustment is the process of developing representations that more accurately reflect the new reality, and allow us to act on the basis of that reality, rather than what used to be true. In short, they work better in this new context.[26]

And the practical implications of that are:

- Be aware of the range of mutually contradictory beliefs you may have on one subject; you can acknowledge they're all there, but choose to go with the one that seems most useful or relevant.
- You don't have to utterly disprove and discard an unhelpful or outdated belief – time may be better spent focusing on a more helpful or accurate alternative.
- If an older, more unhelpful idea pushes its way in, try not to overreact, telling yourself that you're back to square one, or that you were wrong to be more positive. Recognise that the unhelpful idea was bound to be there all along, lying dormant – so long as you don't start

feeding it by going over and over it in your head and agreeing with it, or fighting hard to disprove it, you can choose to focus on the alternative beliefs.

- There's benefit in just recognising that these thoughts are simply that – thoughts. They may or may not be accurate, but when lying awake in bed at 3 in the morning, it's not actually a confrontation with your boss that's interfering with your sleep, but a *thought* about a confrontation.

> It takes a long while for Anil to accept the conclusion that his relationship with Sarah is unlikely to survive. Even now, he sometimes finds himself reacting to a minor positive event – a kind word or a smile from her – by reawakening his belief that they actually have a fundamentally strong relationship that could weather any difficulties. And as pleasant as it is to indulge those thoughts, it makes the pain even worse when reality comes crashing back in. Eventually, he starts to recognise his 'the relationship is fine' belief when it pops up, and steers well clear of dwelling on it.

## Acceptance

And what of acceptance – that Holy Grail-like goal of models such as the one we discussed before? That could be parodied (as *The Simpsons* did) as a calm, smiling statement of 'Oh well, we've all got to go some time!', and one use of the word acceptance is ceasing to fight against the event and recognising its inevitability. It can be hard, though, to distinguish that from fatalism or even helplessness, which can both be uncomfortable states, often associated with low mood or depression.[27] If we argue that acceptance is different, because the person is happy with the change, then I suspect it's a very rare state indeed for the kind of personal disasters we're focusing on in this book. Who would genuinely be happy about bankruptcy and jail?

Maybe it's best to see acceptance as part of adjustment. While the underlying representation hasn't caught up with reality, then there's a temptation to see the past as the norm, and the current situation as a deviation from it. For example, the man who has lost his hair still regards the 'real' him as the one with hair – this new version is an aberration. Acceptance would have happened when he looks at his reflection and says, 'Yes, that's the real me. I used to have hair, but the bald chap in the mirror is who I actually am now.' So, acceptance is about resetting what constitutes normal. We might not be happy with how things are now, and we might be trying hard to work around the changes, but we've stopped spending time pretending or wishing it wasn't true. And we saw in the prevous section that adjustment is beginning to live your life according to that reset version of normality.

We can't just think about acceptance of facts or thoughts, though. Acceptance crucially also involves acceptance of how we feel – even (maybe especially) the unpleasant feelings like sadness, fear or anger. We'll talk more in Chapter 9 about the role that developing an attitude of 'acceptance of how things are' (including acceptance of strong emotions) can help us cope with major distress.

So, does this mean that everyone eventually reaches acceptance? Absolutely not.

## Denial

Commenting on an earlier draft of this book, a friend pointed out the paradox of having a section on handling denial; if someone reading this book in crisis really is in denial, they aren't going to see how it applies to them! That's a fair point, and to some extent this section is aimed more at readers who are friends or family of someone in crisis. However, as we'll see below, being in denial isn't such an all-or-nothing state as people sometimes imagine, so even the person struggling to face the full reality of the situation may find it useful.

So, what about when a person doesn't accept the reality of what is happening? Or, in terms of the model I've just proposed, when that updating of the representation doesn't seem to happen?

When Helen is first told about her advanced, incurable bowel cancer, she listens carefully, and asks some relevant questions of the doctor. When they get outside the office, her partner Keith doesn't know what to say; he's stunned, and Helen is initially quiet. Eventually, she says (in a lighter tone than Keith would have expected), 'Oh well, that's not too bad – at least they caught it early, so now we can fight it, and we're going to beat it for the kids' sake.' Keith knows that those views are the opposite of what the doctor has said, and assumes she must be 'in shock'. It's another week before they talk in depth about what has happened, and Keith finds himself in the middle of a very complicated conversation; at one moment, Helen is discussing how to sort out their son's needs 'after-wards', and the next moment she's talking about a big holiday to celebrate the day when the cancer is finally cured.

We encounter this kind of situation often in healthcare, and Helen's reaction would most likely be referred to as being 'in denial'. But this kind of behaviour isn't unique to illness.

Having known Debbie all her life, her sister Sue is used to how strong-minded she can be, and how determined she's always been to overcome difficulties; so she's not surprised that Debbie doesn't seem too demoralised about the news of the factory closure. Sue starts to worry when, a couple of weeks later, Debbie is continuing as if nothing were happening; she doesn't seem to be making any plans for alternative action, changes the subject if the factory closure is discussed, and even mentions her hopes for promotion at work in a couple of years' time.

In each case, friends, family members and those trying to help are left floundering, because it's hard to know how to deal with denial; if we know they've been told the truth, why do they now seem unaware of it? Did it not 'go in', have they forgotten it, somehow blanked it from their mind, or are they just pretending for some reason?

One difficulty here is that there is actually a range of different things that get labelled 'denial'.[28] In addition to those pure cases of denial where someone may genuinely believe that the bad thing is not happening or will not happen, because their mind has been unable to take it in (we'll discuss why this might happen below), it may instead be the case that:

- They've never actually been told; everyone assumes that someone else has broken the bad news to them, but no one actually has. So when they act as if they don't know – because they don't – they are assumed to be in denial.
- They might have a genuine memory problem (such as early dementia, or a previous head injury).
- They may simply have failed to understand what they've been told (still, sadly, a possibility with complex medical diagnoses, and no doubt common too in legal, financial and other non-medical areas).
- They may understand what they are being told, but think that the other person has made a mistake.
- They may believe part of the news, but not its implications – so someone might accept that their partner is having an affair, but not that their relationship is under threat.
- They may have accepted the news, but have decided to cope by not dwelling on it, and trying to continue with life as normal.
- They may accept that the bad news is true, but be trying to put on a show to others. Perhaps they are hoping to avoid upsetting them, or avoid becoming upset in front of others, or are trying to avoid difficult conversations that they don't want to have.

There are no doubt other examples of 'things that look like denial'; the trouble is that from the outside it can be hard to tell which is going on inside someone.

But leaving aside those 'things that look like denial', what is actually going on where a person has genuinely become unaware of a really important piece of information that they have been told, understood and should have been able to retain?

Inevitably, there are many different types of explanation. Broadly speaking, some of those explanations see denial as a defence mechanism; it's a way of shutting out things that the mind simply doesn't want to be true. Unfortunately, as the evidence for what's really going on mounts up, then it becomes harder and harder to maintain that defence, until the point at which it begins to crumble, or indeed comes crashing down catastrophically. By this view, denial of major events is more or less doomed to fail – and indeed is sometimes referred to as a 'failing defence'.[29]

Another approach argues that denial is (or can be) a way of gradually allowing an awful truth to sink in; rather than taking on board the full reality, and risking being overwhelmed by its awfulness, the truth is kept at a sort of mental arm's length, and gradually dripped in. One writer on this subject described this process as a 'dosing mechanism'. The benefit of this would be that the person can carry on functioning while all the changes are happening, rather than cracking up entirely in the face of the new reality.[30]

There is another possible explanation, which comes from that idea of different, incompatible beliefs coexisting, but at any one moment one dominates the other (remember the example of getting used to the indicator stalk in a new car, and ending up washing the windscreen at someone in anger). This would suggest that some episodes of denial are actually that the belief 'nothing is wrong' is for the time being calling the shots, and the belief that 'I have cancer' or 'I'm going to lose my job' is being suppressed by it, so isn't able to be thought about or expressed. However, it's still there and able either to 'pop up' unexpectedly (like Helen suddenly talking about Liam's future before going back to talking about having her cancer cured), or gradually become dominant so that the 'nothing is wrong' belief fades to the background – though that too may occasionally pop up. This view of denial doesn't see it as either there to help or hinder – it's just a side-effect of how our brains work.

However we see denial working, it's still tricky knowing how to deal with it in those around us.

Sue thinks long and hard about how to deal with Debbie's denial regarding the factory closure. Things need to be planned for the closure – perhaps looking for other work, certainly looking at financial commitments (there's a holiday planned that surely she won't be able to afford now). Should she go along with discussion about the future as if she too thinks nothing is about to change? Should she try to avoid any such conversation? Or should she confront her with the truth?

The person who is apparently in denial provides one of the consistently trickiest communication challenges for those of us working in palliative care, and the same will be true if you encounter it in other walks of life.

Taking the options Sue was considering, colluding with Debbie's fantasies may feel wrong, because it's reinforcing a falsehood, and doesn't move her towards addressing increasingly urgent actions. Just avoiding the conversation may make Sue seem distant and uninterested, and doesn't get Debbie closer to sorting things out. But forcing her to confront the truth might seem like taking away all hope, and might provoke some sort of crisis in Debbie – the worry would be that, if Debbie *still* isn't willing to face up to it, she might simply withdraw from those, like her sister, who are telling her things she doesn't want to hear. And that would further rob her of support.

What that tells us is that there's no one right way of helping someone who appears to be in denial. But if you find yourself having to decide how to deal with such a situation, here are a few things you can bear in mind:

- Try to find out what they do know; maybe ask them to clarify the real picture for you. This should help reveal genuine misunderstandings, or perhaps show that the person knows perfectly well what's going on.
- Try to establish what they see as the best case or worst case, not which of those they see as most

likely. This should help clarify whether the person is simply choosing to dwell on the more optimistic possibilities.

- If their words suggest that they are in denial, consider whether their actions match them; sometimes people will say that things are definitely going to be OK, but their actions suggest they are making the right preparations for things going badly.

- If words and actions both suggest the person really is in denial, your next question should be 'How much does it matter?' If the consequences of the unrealistic belief are not going to be catastrophic, you might decide to just let things develop in their own time.

- If it still looks as if you're going to have to intervene, consider whether there are others you can compare your perceptions with – other friends or family members. Maybe the person you're worried about talks differently to them, or they have information or suggestions that will help you. You could always see what they think about the idea of challenging the denial. If nothing else, there's then a chance of some solidarity if the person in question reacts against you when you challenge them.

- If you are going to challenge the denial, try to go about it gently; the presence of denial about serious issues always means that strong emotions are not far away. After all, if I'm going to the effort of pushing something aside because I don't want to look at it, I'm not going to be thrilled when you shove it under my nose! So don't be surprised if your intervention is met with resistance. What can *sometimes* work is an expression of concern about the situation, then an acknowledgement of the benefits of being positive by looking at the better possible outcomes, before suggesting it might be a good idea to see whether there's anything that needs doing *just in case* the outcome isn't so good. That way, the person isn't being forced to admit they were wrong or foolish, but the 'truth' (whatever that is) has at least been put into the arena.

- If you are rebuffed, try not to get into an argument; if you do, the other person is likely to defend and justify their position. The more they do that, the more they're digging in to their position, so arguing can actually have the effect of strengthening the very opinion you're trying to move them away from.[31] The very fact of raising the topic may gradually have an impact on the other person by strengthening that 'accurate' view that has been suppressed; with time, it may be more able to fight for dominance within that person's mind.

- Although this 'softly softly' approach is usually best, there may be times when the dangers are too great and too imminent to have the time for it, and you'll decide you have to risk a more direct confrontation. All you can do is be clear about *why* you're doing this, try to prepare your arguments clearly in your head beforehand, attempt to remain calm even if you meet fierce resistance, and not allow yourself to get drawn into personal criticism, or distracted by criticisms from the other person. It may not be comfortable, but if there's no alternative, there's no choice!

No matter how clearly we have made sense of and accepted our situation, there will still be difficult choices to be made, and that is what we will address next.

## Key points

- People can go through many stages in getting used to a big change in life, but don't expect those stages to be predictable.
- Successful adjustment might involve changes in outlook, behaviour, relationships and beliefs.

- Beware of trying to make everything the same as it was before: you'll probably fail, you'll be constantly comparing how things are now to how they were, and you may end up causing new problems.
- Adjustment is not about going back to how things were before the change, it's about getting used to a 'new normal'.
- Even when we have got our heads around the new reality, our old ideas about how things are still lurk in our brains, and can pop up unexpectedly, particularly when we're under pressure.
- There are many reasons why the truth might not 'sink in', and it's sometimes part of a healthy process of gradual adjustment.
- If you're dealing with someone apparently in denial, the first question should be 'How much does it matter?' If it does matter, approach the subject carefully (suggestions in the chapter above).

# 5

# What should we do?

## Making decisions

### The importance of control

We are making decisions the whole time. Tea or coffee. BBC or ITV. Sit on the chair or the sofa. Scratch that itch with the left hand or the right – or not at all. Many of these decisions are unnoticeably small, and their consequences are slight. Other decisions may seem small, but can have enormous consequences ('Can I overtake that lorry before the bend?').

In addition to the consequences, big or small, the very act of making decisions appears to have some benefits from the sense of control it gives. Humans (and many other animals) generally dislike feeling helpless and lacking in any control over events. I could point to the current political fashion for seeing choice in services (be that hospitals or TV channels) as being more important than their quality. Or, we could look at the number of lottery and similar gambling activities where the punter is given lots of choices to make (e.g. choosing numbers), when in reality all selections have exactly the same probability of success.

These may simply be reflections of the need for control and for predictability that we've touched on before (e.g. Chapters 2 and 3); a very good self-help book for those recently diagnosed with cancer is called *44½ Choices You Can Make If You Have Cancer* (details in Further Reading near the end of the book), and aims to dispel the sense of helplessness and lack of control some people experience on receiving a diagnosis.

Yet, just as people differ in how much information they want about a bad situation, they also differ in how they want to be involved in decisions.

In healthcare, we've tried to move away from what gets termed 'paternalism' – the doctor, for example, simply making a decision on behalf of the patient – 'in their best interests'. In theory at least, the ultimate decision rests now with the patient, with the professional's role being more one of providing the information which allows the patient to make an informed choice. And here we meet the question of individual differences again: some people really like that way of making decisions, where they have complete control. For some, though, this feels much less comfortable; colleagues of mine often hear variations on the line 'You're the expert, Doc: I want you to make the decision', or 'What would you want if it was you, your child or your mother in my position?' And you can see the point: these can be quite literally life-and-death decisions, and people may feel that, even with plenty of information about the pros and cons of different options, they just don't have the background to make a judgement. Perhaps the way to look at this is not that people are avoiding a decision, but rather they are making a reasoned choice to delegate that decision to their doctor. Actually, given that the person ultimately has to give consent to any treatment, the final decision will still be theirs, even if that is only to accept or reject the recommendation they are given.

And as with information choices, people can differ in how much control they want over decisions, some wanting more autonomy, others less. There are no hard-and-fast rules about who will prefer which, though there is some research suggesting that people who are younger and better educated are slightly more prone to want more personal control.[32] Crucially, though, people are not fixed in all this; on one day, for one decision they may want total control, and on another day for another decision, want someone else to take charge. And it's not always the case that people struggle more with big decisions than small ones; people will frequently make some of the biggest decisions (e.g. whether or not to go ahead with risky surgery) far more quickly than they'd be able to choose a meal from a take-away menu.

Now, it's not just the amount of control that people differ on; it can also be the types of things that influence them. One person may be very averse to risk, so tend to go for the 'safest' option, while another will prefer to take a chance on a riskier option that might just give a bigger payoff.[33]

> When Peter is told that he will indeed be charged with fraud, he finds himself faced with a dilemma: should he plead guilty to the fraud charges in the hope of a lesser sentence, or plead not guilty, running the risk of a longer sentence but with at least the possibility of walking free? The few people he trusts enough to discuss this with seem to vary in their advice. He endures many sleepless nights before reaching a decision.

## How people make decisions

So are there any common factors in how people make decisions? Well, yes in general terms – you might never be able to predict exactly how one specific person is going to react, but we know some of the things that people in general take into account in deciding to do things.

The first is the balance of costs and benefits of a course of action, and how much each of those means to you. So, if we take 'giving up smoking' as an example, the influences may include (perceived) benefits: 'I might not die young' (matters a lot), 'I'll be better off financially' (matters quite a bit), but costs include 'I'll miss the reassuring feeling of a cigarette when I'm stressed' (matters quite a bit), 'I'll lose my cool rebel image' (matters only a little – getting too old for that). Some people think that's the end of the story – weigh the pros and the cons, and whichever wins is the decision. But that's not so, because at least two other major things play a part.

The first is the influence of other people who matter to you; that could be a partner, friends, your doctor, or even people in the media you look up to. In the smoking example, it could be that family and professionals are very keen for you to quit (and they matter quite a bit), but all your mates will think you're boring if you give up, and your idols smoke too (and maybe they matter a lot to you). These particular influences get called the 'subjective norms' and it's not hard to see why public health initiatives (against smoking, or drink-driving, or unsafe sex) work so hard to challenge those behaviours being shown positively in the media – because they genuinely do influence the decisions people make.

The other major influence on decisions is how far you feel able to carry out the behaviour in question – so if you absolutely and genuinely believe you are incapable of giving up smoking (or drinking, or injecting heroin) then it doesn't really matter how clearly you see the benefits of doing so, or how many other people are encouraging you to do it, because it won't appear to be worth trying, as you consider yourself doomed to failure.

Unlike the other influences we've talked about, this one requires knowledge of the exact steps to be taken, because something can appear impossible at first glance, but when broken down into stages can start to look achievable, and so worth going for.

In the middle of all his domestic worries, Anil was unexpectedly offered a promotion. His boss had been impressed with his work on recent projects, and thought he might be the right person to step into a sudden vacancy as manager of one of the teams. Anil was very pleased at this high praise, but – remembering sound advice he once heard to 'never let yourself be flattered into a crap job' – asked for time to think it over. He could see that the benefits of career advancement, higher salary and a more varied workload probably outweighed the downsides of longer hours and more responsibility. Friends and family he asked were unanimous that he should go for it. The problem was that, while he knew he understood the business well and reckoned he could put together great projects, he really doubted that he'd be able to manage other people. He went to his boss to explain this was why he wouldn't be taking the promotion, but instead his boss put together a plan involving going on a 'people management' course, and setting up fortnightly meetings with an experienced team manager to support and advise him on that side of things. With that in place, Anil felt able to take the new job on, and accepted it gratefully.

This way of looking at what shapes our choices has a lot of research backing it up: of course it's just one way of looking at it, and other things can also influence a decision – but it turns out that this approach, called the theory of planned behaviour,[34] is good at explaining lots of different choices that people make, and can also help the person who's really stuck with a decision; it won't necessarily make the choice for them, but it can clarify the reasons for why they're struggling, and maybe point them towards what they need to address to get on with it.

---

**Try this now:**

Think of a choice you're facing, or have faced in the past. Now write down on a piece of paper:

1  All the advantages of the course of action, and how much each matters to you.
2  All the disadvantages of the course of action, and how much each matters.
3  What do significant others (family, friends, professionals) want you to do, and how much each matters to you.
4  Whether you believe yourself capable of going through with the action if you choose to try.

---

Of course, the element of 'how much each matters to you' is going to depend on your personal priorities and values; we'll discuss those in some depth in subsequent chapters.

I said earlier that enormous decisions are sometimes taken faster than trivial ones. Sometimes, though, when you are faced with dire events, decisions can be very difficult to make. There are several reasons why this can be so, including decreased control and decreased predictability.

### Decreased control

The situations we're looking at in this book are inevitable ones – we're focusing on things that we can't prevent. Obviously then we can't at this stage control whether they happen or not (whether, if we had our time over again, we could prevent them is another question). But more broadly, situations like these often involve other people, and other systems (legal systems, healthcare systems and so on). That introduces a whole range of people and things we cannot ultimately control, so the choices we make do not totally decide the outcome. Imagine the differences between planning a holiday for just yourself, and planning a wedding with 200 guests – the wedding will probably involve far more compromising and unforeseen outcomes.

### Decreased predictability

There have been lots of good experiments about how people make decisions.[35] For excellent scientific reasons they often study very simple decisions like 'Would you choose a gift of £100 now, or £200 in six months' time?' The trouble is, most of the important decisions aren't quite as clear-cut as that: consider 'Should I buy this car, which is cheaper but will probably break down sooner, and will be fairly cheap to mend when it does, or that car, which costs more, is more reliable, but costs more if it does need repairing?' Suddenly, we're dealing with far less certain outcomes – the options are less predictable. And for the really big situations we're considering, it can be worse still.

At one of her appointments, Helen's consultant shows her the result of her latest scans, revealing further spread of her cancer. He says that one area of spread is probably responsible for the extra tiredness, lack of appetite and jaundice she's started to experience. He tells her that a specialist at a national centre is trying out a new drug for such cases. But (seeing the sudden gleam of hope in her eyes) adds that it isn't straightforward; if successful, the drug should improve her symptoms, and might add a few months to her life. However, it doesn't work for everybody, gives side-effects that range from short term and minor through to long term and horrible, and would require a long journey to London every three weeks for the injection and monitoring. Seeing how bewildered Helen is by the decision, Dr Vickery suggests that she go home to think about it and come back next week. But when the next appointment comes around, she tearfully explains that she's gone over and over it in her head, but can't decide; she feels well and truly stuck.

## When you're stuck

People are sometimes referred to me because they are at a total loss about how to proceed with a decision regarding their treatment or plans. There can be many reasons for this, but a common one is being 'paralysed by uncertainty'. Many of the important facts about the different options facing them are uncertain: Will the cancer definitely come back? Will it be sooner or later? Would that treatment cure me? Which symptoms will I suffer, and how badly? So, they feel incapable of making a decision, as they cannot know for sure which of the many possible outcomes will actually happen. This leaves them feeling completely stuck, incapable of moving forward, and often increasingly frustrated at their situation.

### Conditional planning

Sometimes, you can get past this by 'conditional planning'; if you don't yet know whether 'a' will happen, or 'b', or 'c', that doesn't mean you can't plan ahead. So long as there aren't too many options, you could try planning for each (If it's 'a', then I'll do this . . ., if it's 'b' then I'll do that . . .); this way, whenever it becomes clear which of the possibilities is actually coming true, you already know what you're going to do (rather than only starting to plan at that point). Anyone who's played sport has probably done that: 'If they take the kick-off long, I'll catch the ball and pass it; if they kick it short, I'll let Steve take it and drive forward.' That works a lot better than waiting until the ball's been kicked, then starting to think, 'OK, it's gone long; now, what's the best thing for us to do . . .?' When applied to really serious decisions (not that getting the restart at a rugby match right isn't serious), this means that you can do preparatory work for each of the options. Naturally, some of that work will end up being wasted (because that option didn't come about), but you have the practical benefit of being prepared for what comes up, and also you have the psychological benefit of feeling on top of things despite the uncertainty of the future.

Actually, sometimes (though by no means always) it doesn't matter too much exactly what the outcomes might be – what you can do next is worthwhile whatever happens. A good example from palliative care is making sure your will is in order; that's essential if you're likely to die soon, but is also a pretty good move if you're around for longer. If nothing else, it's one less thing to worry about.

Helen still can't decide whether to try the new treatment. Should she grab the chance of getting back the appetite and energy to do more with her family (and look a bit less yellow)? But what if she ends up with side-effects that are worse, and uses up lots of her remaining energy on night-mare journeys to London every three weeks until she dies?

Seeing that she's getting nowhere, Dr Vickery suggests that she go to London once and talk it through with the specialist; she could withdraw at any point, and if nothing else she'll have had someone else look at her scans and maybe come up with some different suggestions.

As that approach doesn't seem to close off any options, she agrees, and sleeps a lot better that night.

Actually, we have to be a little careful here: weighing up the pros and cons of actions does make it sound as if people are always rational decision-makers; yet many decisions are made much faster, without much thought (maybe on gut instinct), and we make up a good reason for it later.[36] I suspect we've all found ourselves doing that – coming up with a whole list of sensible reasons why we ought to buy that new computer/shoes/holiday, when it's all really a justification for having fallen for it straightaway. The point is that they aren't so much excuses we come up with to tell other people – we actually tell ourselves they're the real reason for the decision, when in truth they're a story we've made up after the decision's already taken.

### Getting bogged down

But even if we do sometimes make very rapid decisions, it's also true that some people find themselves utterly stuck, going over all the options time and again, getting no nearer to a solution. Although the tendency is to keep worrying at a problem until a solution emerges, sometimes the more often you think of it, the less likely you are to make a decision. I think of it as cart-tracks across a field: the more often our mind follows the same path, the deeper the 'ruts' it leaves, so that next time we're in that field our mental wheels are more likely to follow the same path, and in so doing make it even deeper, meaning next time we're more likely still to be stuck following the same track.

And how can we get unstuck? Well, one way is to talk to someone in some depth about your choices; someone who isn't going to tell you what to do, or even simply sympathise and agree that you can't win; someone who will listen closely and question your thinking, making you put into words your ideas and assumptions, and maybe help you spot any gaps in your information or reasoning. Something as simple as this can be enough pressure to force your wheels out of the same tracks, and maybe you can find a slightly different path to follow.

That kind of conversation is one way of dealing with stuck decisions, but there are others too.

### *Rules of thumb*

There are certain strategies for making decisions that we can use – rules of thumb if you like (the technical term being 'heuristics').[37] Clearly, they're not going to guarantee the best possible decision under all circumstances, but they may allow you to reach a decision that's good enough, and reasonably quick. People actually develop their own rules of thumb, for better or worse (e.g. 'I'll bet on the horse whose jockey is wearing green'); a colleague of mine used to reduce her choices on large items like washing machines by choosing a reasonably priced store, then getting the second most expensive one they had. Similarly, I once heard about a shop which stocked only three examples of things: so they sold T-shirts and their range was just three – a budget one, a luxury one, and one in-between – then it was the same for hi-fis, beds and so on; apparently, they were popular among those suffering choice overload. Interestingly, most of their customers were said to be men.

Here are some strategies that can help; some are well known in research on decision-making, and some have just developed in my clinical practice.

### *Satisficing:*

This is the complete opposite of the old adage 'never make your choice without walking the full length of the counter'. Satisficing (from *satisfactory*) means have in mind what you want from your choice,[38] and instead of exhaustively looking at every available option and trying to weigh up which is absolutely the best choice, simply select the first one that meets the criteria you set, and then stop looking. It means that you run the risk of subsequently seeing an even better option when it's too late, but means that you make your choice more quickly and should still come out with what you wanted from the situation. Some people can't do this, they're particularly prone to what gets called 'anticipated regret' – the prospect of making a choice which they might regret later shapes their behaviour. That sometimes affects people's health-related decisions; they really don't want to try some new treatment, but go ahead anyway for fear that they'll regret it if the illness returns later.

To use satisficing, though, it helps to know what you actually want, and what you'll settle for if that's not available. And working that out will help you no matter what your strategy.

### Go for the best

Choose the option that offers the biggest potential payoff, even if the odds are low and the costs great. It's the equivalent of mortgaging everything you own to invest in that business idea that might make an absolute fortune, but runs a strong risk of failing.

### Avoid the worst

Focus on the drawbacks of the different options; go for the one that avoids the worst outcomes if it goes wrong, even if the gain is small and the risk of failure small. This way, someone might prefer yet another holiday in Grimtown-on-Sea, because at least it avoids the small possibility of earthquakes or volcanoes if they went to Hawaii.

### And when there's nothing to choose between the options

Sometimes, the different options are just so evenly balanced that you can't find any way to judge between them – that's another way that a person can end up getting stuck. It may be that you can get away without making a decision at all, or maybe put it off for a specific period (an hour, a day, a month, a year). But if you have to make that decision, and there's no way of deciding between options, then maybe you have to tell yourself that it doesn't matter which you choose, for if there had been an obviously right one, you'd have spotted that by now, so go ahead and pick either. And if you can't even do that, then do it at random – toss a coin, roll a die. Mind you, that's not always possible if there are others around. One trick I've learned is that, if you wear a watch with a seconds hand, you can make a pretty random decision like this: if there are two choices, then the section of the watch face between 12 and 6 is choice 'a', and the section between 6 and 12 is choice 'b' (if there are three choices, then the sections will be 12–4, 4–8 and 8–12). Allocate those in your mind's eye, then look down at your watch – whichever zone the second hand is pointing at, that's your choice. If you were so evenly balanced in your decision, any one is as good as the other(s). Occasionally, choosing 'a' will make you realise you really wanted 'b' all along. Fine – that's your result. If you then start thinking, 'Yeah, but on the other hand . . .', you're getting into serious indecision, so just stick to the one your watch chose for you.

## Getting it wrong

A word on getting it wrong: sometimes, it will turn out that you have made the wrong choice. And it's easy to jump to the conclusion that you were at fault to do so. Now, if any reasonable person would have realised *at the time* that this was a stupid decision, you were indeed at fault. However, if, on the basis of the information at hand at the time, there was no reason to know that it was the wrong choice, then there was nothing wrong with your decision-making process, even if events do later turn out badly. That might sound pointlessly abstract, but it actually matters, because when people make the wrong decision, and bad things happen as a result, they can end up blaming themselves even if there's no rational reason to do so, and carry that guilt for years to come.

As the factory closure looms, Debbie is getting desperate about finding a new job. Then she sees an article in a local newspaper about someone she used to know who now has a successful business. Three years ago that woman had left the same factory with a mad idea to set up a business making hand-finished ladies' underwear. She had asked Debbie to join her (knowing Debbie to be a better seamstress), but there didn't seem to be a business plan and it wasn't clear who'd want to buy such expensive items. Debbie had decided it would be crazy to leave a steady job with a reasonable salary when she had home and family commitments, and declined the offer. Today, her former workmate's business is booming, and Debbie is about to be jobless. For a week or so, she feels sad and guilty: if she'd made a better decision back then, she wouldn't be in this fix now. It takes a while for her to accept that the other decision would (probably) have been better, but given what she knew at the time, it would have been an irresponsible risk to take. And she has no intention of suddenly following rash whims just because the cautious option has turned out badly in this case.

So, a decision may turn out to be wrong, but if it was the best decision you could have made *at the time*, then don't beat yourself up about it.

### Living for today versus facing the future

To an extent, most decisions are about the future, even if it's a very short-term future (e.g. tea or coffee). In the catastrophic situations we're thinking about here, some of our decisions have particularly big implications for what happens next and, as we have already seen, have lots of uncertainty attached to them. Many of the possible outcomes can be pretty grim, so it's understandable that people can shy away from thinking about the future altogether; it's a strategy you hear a lot – just living for today or living one day at a time. Back when I worked in HIV, before any of the treatments we now have were available, I met a lot of young guys facing a grim future, who coped by basically partying and trying not to think about what came next. Having a limited future certainly can concentrate the mind on making the most of the present. The trouble is, though, that basing decisions entirely upon the current moment can actually prevent you from getting the most out of life. For instance, if you don't think ahead to summer, you won't plan a holiday, and when July comes you're missing out. For those with a longer future, a similar argument could be used for pensions. Yet, thinking only about the future, when that future is uncertain or short, risks neglecting today.

The analogy I sometimes use with people is of walking across a cow field. If you spend all your time watching where you place your feet, you might avoid the cowpats, but you'll end up wandering erratically around, and never make it to the gate. Yet if you focus on the gate, you'll walk through a lot of cow dung en route. The secret is to look up from your feet often enough to keep track of your direction, and your goal. In practice, that means in time of crisis focusing a lot of attention on getting by from day to day, but also occasionally thinking ahead to the future, and checking whether there's anything you ought to be doing to prepare ahead – or maybe if there's anything you might one day really regret not having done.

Of course, what people actually choose to do when they hear that time may be short is not necessarily what they would have thought they'd do. That's sometimes because, at the point it becomes clear that their condition is terminal, they might be so unwell that their choices are limited. But even for people who are in good shape, and have the means, it's quite rare for people to go on a world cruise, or go to see the pyramids. Some may make a trip to see family overseas, but in my experience people choose to do far more simple things – putting their energy into maintaining as normal a family and working life for as long as is possible. Sometimes that may be a financial necessity, or simply being too ill to do anything too ambitious (or to be able to get travel insurance). But many times it's because people are prioritising the things that matter to them, and that they might be about to lose.

There's a really important point here about how bad we tend to be at predicting what we're going to want in the future: early on in their illness, people may have strong opinions about what they would want if offered certain treatments, or what they want if they become too ill to care for themselves. Yet, when they actually get to that situation, they may make a very different choice from what they predicted. That's one of the reasons we have to be so careful about living wills or advance directives requesting that treatment should be withheld if the person becomes too ill to act for themselves. When you're still fit and well, the idea of being stuck in bed and unable to care for yourself might not sound like a life worth living; yet, when a person actually gets to that position, they'll often fight with all their remaining energy to, say, be in their own bed, looking out of their own window rather than in hospital. Suddenly, that bedbound existence seems worth fighting for, even though they'd never have thought that while they were well. I think that's one of the main reasons for the big difference between how many people say they'll kill themselves before they reach the last stages of their illness, and how many actually do.[39]

So how does this (rather gloomy) material about reactions to death relate to those impending disasters that *aren't* about terminal illness? Well, as we have seen repeatedly so far in this book, there's a parallel between facing death and facing other crises; many of the influences, the choices and the mental processes are fundamentally the same, and we can learn from them. In this case, we can learn that our ability to predict our future preferences can be inaccurate, and so it may be important not to commit ourselves to a choice ahead of time if we can avoid it.

There's one final lesson to learn about decision-making from all this, though. One of the very hardest decisions any relative can be faced with is whether to turn off the life-support of someone they love who has been seriously injured or is gravely ill, when there are no prospects of recovery. Or similarly, when a person has declined into a state so near death that it wouldn't be right to attempt resuscitation if their heart stopped.

Except, in the vast majority of cases, that's not actually the relatives' decision. As things stand at the moment in the UK, if an adult is incapable of making a decision (due to being unconscious), then unless there is a prior legal arrangement to nominate someone else to take decisions for them, the decisions will fall to the healthcare team – probably ultimately the consultant doctor – in what they see as the best interests of the patient. The team ought to involve close relatives, principally to see if they can work out what the *patient* might have wanted to happen, not what the *relative* wants.[40] In fairness, in the absence of any clear indications of what the patient would want, many doctors will try to take into account any strong feelings of the relatives, but the best interests of the patient are the ultimate basis of the decision.

Well, let's hope that never happens to us. But what's the lesson from that sad situation? That sometimes what looks like a big decision isn't actually our decision. That may be a good thing, or a bad thing, but we can at least then avoid agonising over a non-decision, or feeling guilty about a choice that we never actually made, or being ignorant of who's *actually* calling the shots.

After his first discussion with his solicitor, it's clear to Peter that he will indeed find himself in court on charges relating to fraud. As well as obsessively collecting together and organising every scrap of information he can about his financial activities, and trying to read up on the relevant laws, he becomes especially preoccupied with the type of trial. Would he be better accepting a Magistrates' Court trial, or should he insist on trial by jury right from the start? He lies awake at nights, wondering if he'll get a more sympathetic hearing from (he presumes) an educated, middle-class magistrate who might understand the pressures on an entrepreneur? Or better with a jury of regular people, who might be persuaded that the whole situation was so complicated that he has simply made the kind of mistake any of them might? Weeks of soul-searching eventually lead him to favour the magistrate. He starts to explain his choice to his solicitor at their next meeting, only to be told that this would definitely be Crown Court – Peter has no say in the matter. If only he'd established at the last appointment who decides what type of trial.

**Key points**

- Check that it is actually your decision to take.
- Try to work out what outcome you want to achieve, and what you'd settle for if that's not possible.

- Some of us like to take decisions more than others; and some tend to be more comfortable choosing risky options. If you know what your tendency is, you can reflect on whether you're actually making the best decision, or just the one that's most comfortable or familiar.
- Don't just weigh up the pros and cons of a decision, allow for how likely each is, and then consider what other key people think you should do (whether or not you agree with them). Look carefully at how far you think you'd be able to manage each of the options. And then reconsider each, because your gut decision may not be the right one.
- If there's no way of knowing how events are going to turn out, is there a 'next step' that would suit all the possibilities?
- If you're stuck between decisions, try one of the rule-of-thumb strategies described above – 'satisficing', 'go for the best', 'avoid the worst', or make a random decision if either option is better than not deciding at all.
- Even though you're mainly concentrating on getting through each day, occasionally give some thought to things further ahead to keep you heading in roughly the right direction (remember the cowpats and field gates).
- Be wary of making irrevocable decisions early in a crisis about what will happen later on; your ideas about what you want to do may very well change.
- If a decision turns out badly, but was the best you could make at the time, there's no point beating yourself up about it. By all means try to learn from it, but don't automatically assume that you're bad at decision-making; that way can just make you feel helpless or guilty, and function less well.

# 6

# Keeping going

## Managing 'normal' daily life

### Why a normal life matters

It's true that the prospect of imminent death (or, I'd argue, any other catastrophe) tends to focus the mind. A considerable amount of thought, and maybe action, will be oriented towards it, whether those are generated by the affected person (e.g. constantly thinking about it, searching the internet) or by others (being called to meetings, attending treatment sessions). I often hear people describe having cancer as like a new career, and one that takes up all your time. Going through a messy relationship break-up or awaiting trial can be just the same.

Yet it's only on TV (and not-very-good TV at that) where the crisis becomes the only thing that matters, and everything else is somehow 'on hold'. In reality, lots of other aspects of normal life have to carry on, such as going to work, playing with the children, caring for elderly parents, running into acquaintances, doing household chores and so on.

And not only must these go ahead, but also it's generally very healthy that they do. Successfully engaging with 'normal' activities can bring welcome distraction from oppressive worries, maintain a more positive mood, help avoid feelings of victimhood and bring helpful social contact.

In the first few weeks after her diagnosis, Helen couldn't cope with the demand of the school run, or even just keeping the family home going. Her partner Keith was happy to take most of it over, and Helen realised that he would have to learn to do that in the end when she wasn't around any more. But years as a single mum have bred a strong need for independence, and she's beginning to hate not being 'on top of things' any more. Despite the feeling that she'd rather be sitting somewhere quietly thinking about what's happening, she gradually restarts taking Liam to school, and does the household accounts jointly with Keith. Though each has its challenges, she begins to feel a little more in control, a little less as if her life were now only 'about' her cancer, and she enjoys having a little time when her mind's occupied with normal things.

That's why people are so keen to advise you to 'try to live as normal a life as possible' when facing a crisis. Unfortunately, never has there been a better example of something being easier said than done.

This 'normal life' is made harder to live by the shadow of the crisis in your mind, or the minds of others you meet. That crisis (or its prospect) can affect how you communicate and your relationships with others (colleagues, friends, family and your partner). It raises questions that may not have been there before about your job, your leisure, or your social life. And in addition, it may have a big impact on how much energy you have available.

Let's look at each of those.


**Communication**

Why should living with the prospect of a crisis make communication difficult? There are several reasons:

- You may be so preoccupied with your crisis that you can't concentrate on anything else, because your mind is always elsewhere.
- A strong emotional reaction (being panicky or very depressed) can make you less able to communicate well.

- Other people may want to talk about your problem when you don't; or alternatively, may be completely avoiding mentioning something that's really important to you.

Since the news has broken about the factory closing, Debbie has found meetings at her church quite stressful because her friends keep asking her what she thinks about it, how she's feeling, what she'll do. Most of the time she can see that they're just trying to be caring, but she really wishes they'd let her focus back on setting up the new 'Young Mums' support group; at least that's something where she can genuinely make a difference (unlike the factory closure).

Helen, on the other hand, finds it quite odd that most work colleagues barely mention her cancer. When she returns to work for a while on lighter duties, people seem desperate to talk about anything except what she's going through; the only comments about her health tend to be how well she is looking. When she becomes tearful one day and discusses the situation with her boss, she's told that everyone has been impressed by her determination to return to work given what's happened, and they thought she must be wanting to get back to a bit of normality; to be treated like one of the girls again, rather than a cancer 'victim'. For that reason, her workmates have agreed not to dwell on her illness, but talk about the usual things of work, TV, etc. Helen is shocked and upset by this treatment and gets quite cross with her partner Keith when he points out that they are just trying to help her.

It can actually get a bit easier if you realise that people are sometimes bound to say the wrong thing, take the wrong approach to discussing your situation with you (talk about it too much, too little, too bluntly, or too euphemistically). That isn't usually because they are uncaring or stupid, but mostly because they can't read minds; how Helen wants to be treated is not the same as how Debbie does, and what they want one day may be different the next. But if you tell yourself that everyone else is at fault (for their inability to mind-read), you're going to add anger and isolation to a list of problems that was already bad enough. That doesn't mean you have to just shut up and put up with it; if you find yourself really bothered by others' attitudes, you could try telling them how you'd rather they spoke to you (or didn't) about your situation. Just don't expect that everyone will be able to live up to your ideal.

Helen goes back into work, and tells her colleagues that she'd much rather everyone was open about her cancer. She leads the way by discussing her plans for her funeral, which she speaks of in a matter-of-fact manner, including her opinion of the decor at the local crematorium. What she doesn't notice is that when this type of conversation starts, one of her colleagues always disappears to the toilet, where she cries about the death of the mother she recently nursed through a terminal illness. When others realise what's happening, they have no idea how to reconcile the opposing needs of their two vulnerable friends.

For some people who have been out of circulation (socially or at work) during some sort of crisis, the prospect of being asked about highly upsetting events can be a big barrier when returning. It's not just a question of your closest colleagues; answering the phone to a business contact you only speak to every few months could easily have you being asked 'Where have you been the last few weeks?' You might not want everyone knowing your personal business, you might want to focus on work rather than your troubles, or you might be worried that you'll become distressed in front of these people.

Remember that it's your information, and – for the main part – you can share it with whom you choose, with the level of detail (or honesty!) that you prefer. So, you might want close colleagues to know lots of the detail, then they can support you at rough moments, but just give a more basic explanation to others. If you've had cancer, and been away for months during surgery and chemotherapy, you might choose simply to say, 'I was receiving treatment for a serious condition, but I'm much better now, thanks', and then move the conversation on. Of course, you can't prevent someone failing to take the hint, and asking what kind of illness; but then you have the option of replying something like, 'Actually, I'd rather not go into that; I'm trying to focus all my attention on getting back into the job'.

Now, if you find yourself unexpectedly facing a question you dread, it can be hard to think of the right words there and then. But these events are actually quite predictable, so you have the chance to prepare. For the patients I see who are concerned about these things, I encourage them to come up with an answer (or two or three answers, ranging from single-sentence to more detailed) to being asked about their health, while they are with me in the office. We work on these answers (to make sure they suit the individual's 'style'), and I get them to practise producing them when I ask, and then go home and practise further in the mirror. The whole idea is that, if asked out of the blue, they don't have to start constructing an appropriate answer while they're feeling under stress, because one will be ready to roll off the tongue. And the reason for having several different versions ready is that you may want to go into more detail with some people than with others, and yet still have control over the limits of what you say.

---

**Try this now:**

Take a crisis you're facing, or that you're fearful of, and come up with a brief, prepared answer that does not go into any more detail than you would want to disclose. Then practise it in the mirror; it helps to actually hear the words coming out of your mouth. Also practise ways of dealing with intrusive follow-up questions, preferably without being aggressive or making the other person feel bad (unless that's the effect you want!)

You may have noticed that I started that section by saying that 'it's your information, and – for *the main part* – you can share it with whom you choose'. We've got to recognise that, as useful as it is to manage the information you pass on, sometimes it's politic, or even legally necessary, to go into more detail. Examples of this include:

- Conversations you have with your advisers (doctors, lawyers, accountants, who may not be able to advise you properly if they are given only part of a story.
- Legally binding documentation, such as insurance proposal forms or job applications. Obviously, people do sometimes 'spin' – or downright lie – on these forms, but we have to remember that the penalties can be severe, be they dismissal from a job, an insurance company refusing to pay up on a policy where your application was misleading, or actual legal proceedings.

## Work

Given the dilemmas about communication in the work-place, it's worth reminding ourselves why people work at all. The answer is usually simple – to earn money. So, many people in crisis will need to continue working, or get back quickly to work if that is at all possible.

Yet someone may be signed off sick, or be in a position to have some sort of leave of absence from work. Then there are decisions to be made about whether you want to be off work, or for how long, and these decisions are not always straight-forward. In Chapter 5, we looked at some of the factors that influence people's choices; we can apply them here.

Advantages of work include the following:

- *Normality*: work can bring a sense of normality and of continuity with your previous life. For many of us, work is not just what we do, it becomes part (though usually only one part) of who we are. Getting back to work makes us feel a little like our old selves again.
- *Distraction*: work may also bring welcome distraction from the concerns of our situation. When our minds are not occupied, the most significant thing around may well

dominate. In the face of major changes, it can be a relief to have to focus on work tasks instead of our worries and the uncertainties of the future. This is especially true given that the crises we're discussing are generally ones we have little control over; it is hoped that some parts at least of our work can give us a sense of mastery and competence.

- *Social contact*: our workplaces may contain friends, or even just colleagues. This can bring the mood-lifting benefits of social contact with people who are probably not associated with the crisis in question.

Disadvantages of work include the following:

- *Stress*: work is not necessarily the haven of support and tranquillity we may hope, and distraction and social contact may drift into pressure and conflict, just adding to the problems.
- *Performance*: worries, pressure, sleep loss and interruptions from events relating to the crisis can impair concentration and thus effectiveness at work.[41] In some jobs with a strong safety component (e.g. pilots, surgeons, people operating complex machinery) this could be sufficiently dangerous to make work unsuitable – possibly unethical – during the crisis. For many others, any decreased effectiveness will be an irritation to themselves, or may at worst bring them into conflict with their employer. With cancer, employers are often fairly understanding; that isn't always the case, especially with less physically based crises, or where there is any element of blame being attached.

  Sometimes, the problem doesn't arise from your colleagues' attitudes to you performing less well, but from your own; we are often our own harshest critic, but time spent fruitlessly criticising ourselves for something we can't help just risks undermining our confidence and motivation even further.
- *Nature of the work*: sometimes, the workplace is where the crisis in question is taking place, meaning you are constantly exposed to the problem.

Debbie had always coped with pressures in life by throwing herself into her work. But now, with the knowledge that the factory was going to close, just being at work was a reminder of what she was about to lose. What's more, her colleagues were so demoralised that it was hard to hear anything but bitter conversations. For the first time in her adult life, she dreaded going into work, even though it was the loss of that work that was getting to her.

Even where the workplace isn't the source of the problem, it can be similar enough to the issue you're facing to prevent you switching off from your concerns. We might see this in a nurse who has recently been bereaved, and finds it hard when caring for patients who remind her of the person she's just lost. Or an accountant who is in a financial crisis, and struggles not to think about that when she's faced with sorting out the books of a failing company.

As was discussed in Chapter 5, we don't actually coolly weigh up the pros and cons of a situation then arrive at the logical decision – gut feeling often plays a pretty big role. Nevertheless, it's still worth thinking through some of the factors outlined above – even gut feelings can be changed by the realisation of 'Oh, I never thought of that . . .'

It's also worth mentioning what happens if, for practical, health or stress-related reasons, you've been off work for a while and are now facing going back. That can be a fairly daunting prospect, but can't usually be put off forever. Indeed, it's as if the dread of returning 'incubates' over time. I think there's then a trade-off between how thoroughly you've recovered from the cause of absence, and how much worse the prospect of return is getting. Return too soon, and you increase the risk of performing very poorly, and of relapsing; delay it too long, and the dread of returning builds up to the point where it's yet another problem you're having to deal with. Just what's the optimum moment will depend on a lot of job-specific and individual factors, but for many people putting off return until they're absolutely 100 per cent over whatever was the problem is unrealistic, because often you're not going to feel back to normal (whatever that now is) until you're back into normal activities.

Where absence has been for health or stress problems, there is often a strong argument for phased returns to work – starting back on shorter and/or fewer shifts than before, building up to whatever is the normal pattern. Many employers offer this, and not just out of the goodness of their corporate hearts; this approach is held to make the returnee less overwhelmed, therefore pick up their performance more quickly, and be less likely to relapse and potentially be off sick again. Given the difficulties of facing people (discussed in the section on 'Communication'), I usually suggest people have a 'social' visit back first – arranged over lunchtime perhaps – to get past the anxieties of setting foot in the place and facing colleagues and their questions before you have to start performing in your work.

Obviously, there are some settings and some individuals where this simply isn't on. Do beware, though, of telling yourself that you can go back full-time, and just 'take it a bit easier' at first. Many people report that, once you're back, you're back; others rapidly forget your state, and your own usual approach to work will quickly re-establish itself, making insufficient allowances for reduced stamina. That's the reason why initially limiting the time spent at work is a far more effective way of allowing readjustment; even if work is still pretty full-on, at least it's not as long until you're able to rest and recover again. We'll look further at stamina and energy later.

## Relationships

### *Friends and colleagues*

We know that having a good network of friends can reduce the effects of stress in life.[42] They can provide distraction, enjoyable events, emotional support and even practical help.

When things work well, at any rate. Problems can occur if you don't have friends because of living in an isolated setting (common both in rural areas and big cities), your own personality or just circumstances; for instance, some people find that after separation or divorce, their former partner seems to have got 'custody' of their joint friends. Also, sadly, as we move into old age, friends of our own age group tend to get thinner on the ground, and no matter how kind younger people are, that's often not quite the same as someone who shared your reference points in growing up and growing older. One general implication of this is that, no matter how busy our work, or strong our devotion to family life, it's healthy to maintain friendships as well.

Yet, even when we start off with a good network of friends, facing a crisis can interfere with those relationships. For instance, our friends may be connected to a certain activity – people we meet up with in the pub every Friday, or members of a motorbike touring club; when we don't have the energy, money, time or inclination to do those activities, we can easily lose contact with those friends. Of course, some may cross over and become friends in a different way (maybe visiting us at home), but that's probably the exception rather than the rule. If we no longer have that thing in common which brought us together, there may be little to connect us (or simply to talk about).

It might be a less obvious change that makes a difference. People are used to their friends playing certain roles – being a good listener, or being the one who always organises the outings, or is always good for a laugh. If we stop acting that way, people can find it difficult. If your friends become more distant because of this, it's easy to become angry or bitter, saying that they weren't interested in your well-being, just what they got from you. And that may be true; however, it might also be that they're just feeling unsure how to relate to you, and what you need from them. It's worth trying to be explicit about it, maybe explain that you don't feel up to socialising with lots of people at the moment, but is there any chance of meeting up for a quiet coffee or pint?

What's more, when we're going through difficult times, sometimes we simply don't want to be around others much; we want the space, to avoid having to talk about it, or sometimes we're worried about becoming emotional in front of others. These are all perfectly reasonable instincts, but do bear in mind the positive aspects of involvement with friends described above, and remember that total withdrawal from friendships during a crisis (particularly a long one) might mean those relationships just aren't there to go back to any more once the crisis has passed.

### *Relationships and family*

It's sometimes said that 'friends are the new family'; that a variety of social changes (for instance, people living further away from their parents) have meant that adults today often rely on friends in a way they would have relied on family in years gone by.[43] Even so, for most people family life ends up closer, more important, and often trickier than any other set of relationships. Whether it's parents, siblings, children, stepfamilies, in-laws or extended family members like aunts or cousins, families can be the main source of support, or of stress – and sometimes both simultaneously!

So it makes sense to spend a little time thinking about the impact of facing a crisis on family life. And I think it's important to define 'family' very widely here, because people live in such a range of family settings, from the stereotypical nuclear family of mum + dad + 2.4 children to single parents, childless couples, stepfamilies, extended families living together and even sometimes very close friend groupings. That said, there's little point in discussing each family type in detail, because your relationship with another person is down to a unique combination of the situation and the personalities of each of you, rather than what type of family arrangement you have.

As with friends, we play many roles within family life. Some of them are very practical (like earning money, cooking food, repairing the roof), while others are more emotional (providing love, comfort, reassurance, chastisement). Alongside these, there may be a role of having fun together, and in some relationships being sexual partners. So anything which disrupts the roles we play, or how well we are able to play them, can have a major impact on our lives and those around us.

And living with a crisis certainly can disrupt things. How? Well, we might lack the time or energy to act as normal; we might be too stressed or preoccupied. Also, as we'll discuss further in Chapter 8, when we have strong emotions to deal with (and that's common in crises), our priorities can shift away from seeking pleasure, good relations with others, and sexual interest can certainly decrease.

These changes can have many consequences for us within families, be they practical (bills not being paid, responsibilities not met) or personal (worsening relationships, inability to support others). In some cases, these changes act to compound the problem.

> Anil's relationship worries are eating away at him. The more he thinks about them in Sarah's presence, the quieter and more withdrawn he gets. If challenged on this change, Anil only tells Sarah he's 'fine', which she doesn't believe for a second, but leads her to give up bothering to ask. This makes them more distant with each other. What's more, as Anil gets increasingly down about it all, on the odd occasion when Sarah tries to initiate sex, he finds he has little interest, and can't manage a usable erection. Anil then lies awake convinced that this will make Sarah all the keener to look elsewhere for relationships.

We can see how, in Anil's case, a kind of feedback loop can develop, where the way a person reacts to the initial problem actually increases that problem, which can then strengthen the unhelpful reaction and so on. It becomes really important to stay aware of what the underlying problem is, and what is being added to it by our reactions, because we may not be able to change the underlying problem, but we may well be able to adjust our reactions, and at least stop ourselves from making things even worse! So in Anil's case, he may not be able to get rid of his underlying worries about the relationship, but he could choose to put more effort into time spent with Sarah, rather than withdrawing.

The opposite of that is the possibility of a family (and remember that can be just two people) compensating for the change in one of its members. So, others take over some of the practical tasks, or emotional roles.

> Before her husband Peter's business failure led him into serious financial and legal problems, Alice had always seen herself as the weaker partner in their marriage. She habitually left major decisions to Peter, deferred to his opinion and relied on him to know what to do in an emergency. Yet since he has been facing his current crisis, he has been far more prone to indecision and self-doubt at home. To her surprise, Alice has found that she has become more decisive and confident, able to handle meetings with solicitors, explain matters to relatives and even deal with a local journalist who phones trying to get a story about Peter's case. And while Peter has quickly come to rely on this new Alice, there is part of him that feels even weaker as he sees her get stronger.

Of course, it doesn't always work out that neatly; sometimes, it's just not within the capabilities of other family members to do those things (maybe most people can learn to wire a plug, but not everyone can breast-feed the baby!). Some changes can be managed in the short term, but quickly become too much, particularly if the person doing the compensating still has his or her other responsibilities to attend to. This can lead to difficulties when what *appeared* to be a short-term crisis becomes a long-term or chronic one; the extra work that a partner was happy to shoulder during the crisis becomes more burdensome, and possibly resented, as time drags on. And frustration isn't just experienced by the person who's taking over the responsibilities; despite any good intentions that lie behind another family member taking over some of your duties, it's not unusual for guilt or frustration at not being able to do it yourself leading to resentfulness (however undeserved), and maybe 'pickiness' about how the other person is going about the things you normally do.

Finally, we mustn't forget that other family members are themselves affected by the type of crisis we're considering here; they as well might be too busy, preoccupied or stressed to function to their normal levels, let alone be able to compensate for someone else. Indeed, it's something we often see in cancer and palliative care, that the spouse is more stressed than the person who's ill.[44] We'll discuss some of the reasons why in Chapter 8.

When you hear couples talking about a time of great stress, they'll sometimes speak in terms of 'facing it together', or even that the problem has brought them closer. Even in the best relationships, though, that can't be taken for granted; problems can come between couples (or whole families), meaning that people direct their anger or fear at each other, rather than at the problem. Often, this is because they're inaccurately seeing the *person* as the cause of the difficulties, not the situation. Peter might feel that he's bringing ruin to the family because his business is going under; Helen considers herself a burden on her family because of the care she needs from them when she's ill. In reality, the problem is not primarily Peter, it's the bankruptcy; it's not Helen, it's the cancer. There's a lot less guilt and anger around if we 'name the problem' properly. That's not to say that an individual might not bear some responsibility – their gambling contributed to the financial crisis, their smoking caused the lung cancer – and some anger and/or guilt may be inevitable. But if a family is to find the best way it can through a major crisis, it'll usually do better by identifying the problem (cancer, bankruptcy, redundancy) as the enemy, not each other.

Actually, there's another very important example of 'naming the problem correctly' that I come across all the time in cancer care. Because, by and large, cancer is picked up earlier than it used to be, it's often the case that at the point of diagnosis the cancer itself has not caused any severe symptoms (or maybe no symptoms at all if picked up as a lump at screening or by vigilant self-examination). And straight away, the person may have surgery, or chemotherapy that can cause very strong side-effects over several months – not always, but often. Then the chemotherapy can begin to feel like the enemy, because it's making you feel exhausted, sick or sore, or causing you to lose your hair. The resentment towards the treatment can build up and up, and you can end up feeling like a victim, which is never good for anyone's psychological health. In reality, of course, the cancer itself hasn't given you such symptoms because of the early detection and treatment; left untreated, it would be a different story. I often end up helping patients realise this, and so hang on to the idea that:

> The chemotherapy is not the enemy; the cancer is the enemy. The chemotherapy is the price I choose to pay to fight the cancer.

As I write this, I know those very words are written on bits of paper on fridge doors across Herefordshire! It doesn't make the nausea or fatigue go away, but by correctly naming the problem, any anger is shaped into determination to fight rather than desperation and the desire to give up. And let's hope it's clear how the same could apply to other examples of unpleasant but necessary actions, for example a highly disciplined economy drive that you're trying to implement to sort out a debt problem.

Turning back to family coping, there is one specific problem that we should also watch out for in situations like these, namely *mutual protection*. This is a common thing to see within families; each person is trying to protect others from harm. We could argue that this is one of the basic rules of loving someone – you try to look after them. However, sometimes this valuable instinct can backfire; this is a situation we encounter all the time in palliative care.

Helen counts herself lucky to have a partner as supportive as Keith. If she has an appointment he'll take her there, she barely has to lift a finger at home, and he remains constantly positive. That, however, becomes part of the problem – he is always adamant that 'we'll beat this illness', always seeking the most positive explanation of any symptom, and after sitting in on appointments, recalls only the positive aspects of what the doctor has said, downplaying or ignoring anything negative. It's as if he's switched places with Helen since her initial denial. Inside, he is terrified about what is happening and gloomy about the future, but is utterly determined not to let Helen or their son Liam see it.

Helen too has her share of fears for the future, sometimes wanting to voice them, to talk seriously about what she wants when the end comes, and about Liam's needs after she has died. But she can't bring herself to say any of that to Keith; he seems so certain that everything will be OK that she can't bear to shatter the illusion.

What we are seeing here is a product of the very best intentions backfiring. Each one wants to support and protect the other, but in so doing each is preventing the other from asking for and getting the kind of support they really need – be that the chance to plan for the future, discuss what's really going on, or simply have someone listen sympathetically while they say how awful everything seems right now. A person can end up not only feeling unsupported, but actually being unable to take important action (like having a doctor check out a new lump, or seeing an accountant or lawyer about what would happen if their company is heading for bankruptcy) because it would distress their partner.

Alternatively, you may get to the point where you can't take your partner's constant optimism, and start trying to convince them that the situation really is bad. And what can happen then is that, the more your partner argues that everything really will be OK, the stronger you end up having to argue that, no, it really really is terrible. As in many of these types of arguments, each partner then gets more entrenched in their opinion and ends up believing a more extreme position (whether optimistic or pessimistic) than they initially did. And they argue a lot. Neither of which are what you or your partner set out to achieve.

I've already mentioned that it's part of the deal when we love someone that we do our best to protect them from harm and from hurt. Sometimes, though, protecting them from short-term hurt actually exposes them to more harm, as we've seen above. And we're all capable of being selfish, too; some of that motivation to be constantly positive can be to avoid seeing someone we love distressed – or even to prevent ourselves from having to face our own fears (see section on 'Denial' in Chapter 4).

And if the urge to protect our partners (and ourselves in the process) is a strong one, it's often nothing compared to our urge to protect our children.

> As time goes on, and the closure of the factory gets nearer, Debbie is more and more preoccupied with how she'll manage in the future. Although her 15-year-old daughter Beccy is at the heart of her concerns, she's determined not to burden her – after all she's having to work hard at school, and why give her worries before the disaster has even happened? For her part, Beccy can see that Mum's bothered by something. She knows local factories are always closing (that's nothing new in their town) but Mum's always saying not to worry, her job is safe because she's worked hard, and found a trade and . . . well, that's normally the point Beccy stops listening before it becomes another sermon. No, if Mum's worried it must be something else – another failed attempt at a relationship, or maybe (Beccy particularly fears) she's seriously ill; two of her friends' parents have had cancer, and one died. She can't bring herself to ask Mum outright, and is so scared that Mum's about to announce it that she takes to avoiding her as much as possible and staying out late. Inevitably, there start to be more arguments.

It's really hard telling your children bad news; there are difficult decisions about when to tell them, how to explain in a manner they'll understand, whether there are details best left out for now, how to answer any questions they have.[45] It's also hard to deal with their reaction; it's upsetting having to see them become distressed – worried, tearful, or even angry because of what you've said. As with adults, we can feel as if we've done the harm by telling them the news, rather than understanding that the tears are a product of the bad event, not our telling.

And it's also common, even with very bad news, for children to react in an unnervingly 'matter-of-fact' way; told that their grandma has died, or their parents are separating, they ask if they can go and watch TV because their favourite programme is on soon. It's not that they don't care, but rather that they sometimes don't deal with it all at once – they go onto 'auto-pilot' and do the usual, familiar things while they gradually let the information sink in. But if you're not ready for it, that reaction can seem devastatingly callous.

However, not telling them at all can come at a heavy price; as we saw in Debbie's example, children generally notice when something's amiss, and if they aren't given an explanation of what's actually going on, they'll probably come to their own conclusion, which may be worse, or at the very least lead them to behave in ways that make the situation even harder to bear. In particular, there's a risk that children will think they're to blame for whatever's happening – if told that 'Daddy's gone to a country far away' (when he's actually in prison), a young child might think he's gone to get away from her because *she* was naughty.

---

**Try this now:**

If you are facing a crisis, and if you have children, ask yourself:

- What do you think they know about it?
- How have they seemed to act around you – at all differently from usual?
- Are they carrying on with their normal activities, keeping up with their friends?
- Is there someone else who knows them well enough that you can check out how you think your children are coping?
- Maybe you can bounce ideas off that other person on whether there's anything else you (or someone else) can do to support your children during this crisis.

Returning to the issue of mutual protection, this applies with children as well as partners because in reality children will often try to protect their parents in these situations; they hide their own worries and suffering because they don't want to burden their parents, who are already having a hard time. And the difficult thing as a parent is knowing whether that is happening, because they can be very good at hiding their suffering; even if sometimes we can 'see through' their facade, often we won't. So what can you do?

- Let them know they can tell you if they're worried – don't go trying to prise it out of them, but occasionally remind them that it's OK for them to talk about worries, or ask difficult questions.
- Model the behaviour you desire; without flooding them with your own emotional needs, it's OK to let them see that at times you're worried, or down, or cross about the situation, and explain that to them. That way, they're more able to express the same things themselves, and know they're not to blame for your emotions.
- Identify someone else that both they and you trust – a good family friend, or parent of one of their friends, or an aunt or uncle, say, and ask if they'd be willing to be someone the child can turn to (including voicing their fears, asking questions that they don't want to burden you with). If they would, then you can explain to your child that you realise sometimes it might be hard for them to talk to you (for the reasons outlined above); so, while you're always happy to talk to them about anything, there's also Uncle Billy, or Emma's mum who'd be happy to talk to them. Or maybe with your child it would be better for that other person to approach them and offer. The key thing is that they have a channel for communication and support on these emotional matters, which doesn't depend on them telling you everything on their minds.

We've talked about one special group of family members (children), but we mustn't forget that there may be others who are also strongly affected by what happens to us. Our own parents will have their natural protective instincts, may be worried, and may well end up being starved of information in a different way from our children. Their needs may be different from children's, but they must still be thought about carefully.

## Hobbies and leisure

After talking about matters as important as families, love, and earning a living, it might seem trivial to be discussing hobbies and leisure.

Not so.

The core philosophy of palliative care is that quality of life is what we're fighting for; when people are very ill, they might not be able to do exactly the same things for pleasure that they normally would, but finding something positive to do brings improved mood, welcome distraction (even if only partial) from the problem, and often increases motivation.

And those things are well worth fighting for even in situations where we're not facing life-or-death struggles.

> Since it became clear how much financial trouble Peter is in, he has become totally preoccupied with his case. It seems to his wife, Alice, that every waking moment is devoted to searching the internet, talking to people who might know something about it, writing lists or reading books about financial law. A few times she has gently suggested that it might do him good to spend an after-noon fishing, or go to a cricket match, as he normally finds them both relaxing. Peter answers (more angrily each time) that he has far more important matters to deal with now.

And that's one of the problems; of course, following a hobby, going out for a drink with a friend or playing a sport isn't as important as the crisis you're facing. However, it's also true that the hour or two that any of those would take is unlikely to make any difference to the outcome of that crisis; it's actually likely to be some break from yet more fruitless worry. The problem is therefore generally not one of being *able* to spare the time – it's actually one of *allowing* ourselves to spare the time. And even if we can't bring ourselves to do it for the sake of feeling a bit better, we should be able to do it for the sake of returning to the problem fresher, and more relaxed.

In fairness, though, it's not always so easy to do those leisure things we're used to. In the case of illness, we might not be physically up to it. With other problems, there might come other limitations: we might not be able to afford the cost of the activity any more, it might be hard to get to it, other people might be a barrier (you really can't face them, or they don't want contact with you).

Adding all of these up, the temptation is simply to give up on hobbies or leisure, because you can't do them in the form you would previously, and that can be a loss in all sorts of ways. I remember working with one man who had become very depressed because his advancing illness meant that he wasn't going to be able to teach his son sea-fishing, which had been an important part of his own life and his son was now getting old enough to try it for himself. After careful consideration, it was clear that the man was right; he wasn't going to be able to get on a boat, let alone handle fishing equipment. Even a river or canal bank would be too much for him. So we then looked at *why* it mattered so much to him to be able to teach his son sea-fishing; we worked out that it was a combination of

- spending time together
- teaching his son something that might stay with him into adult life (particularly important as sadly Dad wasn't going to be around for that)
- the fond memories he had of when his own late father had taught him fishing.

So while fishing might not sound very important, and his son could no doubt learn by other means, once we understood why teaching his son mattered so much to this man, we could see that there were some important things among the reasons. As we'll see in Chapter 8, whenever a person's emotional reaction seems out of proportion to the event in question, it usually means we haven't understood what that event *means* to that person.

The first thing we had to do, then, was acknowledge that it was a real loss not to be able to teach his son, and it was understandable to feel sad about it. Not doing that would run the risk of trivialising those important matters of their relationship, how he would be remembered and 'giving' his son something that might be an important part of his future.

We then tried to identify something else that was within his now limited physical abilities, but would still go some way towards meeting the same underlying needs that made him want to teach his son fishing. After some reflection, he settled on teaching him chess instead. He would have preferred it to be fishing but, given that wasn't possible, teaching chess still involved time together, passing on something he had learned from his own father, and giving his son something that (if he wanted) could become a part of his own future.

In a sense, we had to look beyond his initial goal ('teach my son to fish') and find what personal *value* that served for him (something like 'be an important part of the lives of the people I love') and then find a different way of serving that same value. We'll return to this in Chapter 9.

Now, there's an important point to make here: we didn't kid ourselves that this solution made it all OK, and so there was nothing to be sad about. Chess was definitely second best to fishing, and there was still loss there, which deserved some mourning. But, despite the inevitability of that loss, there was still something that could be done to make the situation more bearable, so long as we faced the reality, treated it with some respect, and thought about what we could do despite it. And that, of course, is the philosophy of this whole book.

This does, though, raise another point: we can't rely on other people always fitting in with what we'd choose; the man I've just discussed found his son was actually keen to learn chess, but it might have needed to be something else. When I think of my two sons, each of them has indeed picked up on an interest of mine; the younger spends much of his time playing or watching rugby and the older is fascinated by movies. But trying to make the elder like rugby would have been as futile as making the younger sit through French thrillers of the 1980s – I would have had to find some other point of connection. Once again, by looking at the underlying qualities, we could have found other possibilities if necessary.

So much for a palliative care example; but does the equivalent apply to non-illness crises? Well . . .

As well as feeling guilty for snapping at his wife when she suggested cricket or fishing, Peter realises that he probably does need a break. In reality, 'being too busy' isn't the issue, but either of those pastimes allows too much time for his mind to wander, and probably wander back to his difficulties, so maybe they're best avoided. On thinking about it, he realises that he usually enjoys them because they get him into the open air, don't involve conversation, and don't feel at all rushed; these are clearly what he needs. So his wife, Alice, is pleasantly surprised when she gets home from the shops to find he's taken out his bicycle for the first time in a couple of years, and gone for a ride around the local country lanes.

There's another point worth noting here; when Peter happened to choose a form of exercise as a leisure activity suiting his needs (rather than, say, watching horse-racing) he might have done himself a double favour, because it's now clear that regular exercise is one of the better treatments for mild to moderate depression and anxiety (provided, of course, it's within limits that are physically safe for you).[46] There seem to be some good physical and biochemical reasons for this, but exercise can also improve your self-esteem, give a sense of control and provide a welcome focus away from your problems. One of the most straightforward pieces of advice for coping with adversity, then, is 'Get some exercise!' But if you're planning to do so, spend a little time thinking through what suits you best – exercise can be alone or with others, in a sports setting like a gym or out and about like walking a dog (though it would need to be brisk walking to get the antidepressant effects), and can vary hugely in cost. And, of course, it's also important to consult your family doctor before undertaking any significant increase in exercise.

## Energy

'I haven't got the energy . . .' is one of the main reasons people give for not taking up exercise, or any other activity. Sometimes, of course, that's just another way of saying 'I can't be bothered' – most of us have been guilty of that one at some point! And as a one-off excuse, there's not a lot to say about it, other than the obvious fact that you only get the benefits of activity by doing some.

There's also the problem that depleted energy (and indeed lack of motivation) are common consequences of low mood and depression – and as we'll see later on, those are common enough states among people facing crises. We'll look in Chapter 8 at some of the things that can help with low mood, but while we're talking specifically about energy, we need to be aware of a particular 'trap'. A person who is down will tend to feel less energetic and more apathetic; they'll therefore do less, which includes fewer things that bring either a sense of pleasure, distraction or achievement; this makes them feel worse about themselves, and so they feel more down, therefore they have less energy and so on. And so the vicious cycle continues, intensifying as it goes. The good news is that once a person breaks out of this cycle and starts actually doing things (perhaps using some of the techniques in this book), they find they start getting more energy and motivation, not less.

Yet it's also true that sometimes energy can indeed be in short supply. That's certainly true of some forms of cancer (and/or their treatment), of neurological conditions like multiple sclerosis, and many chronic cardiac and lung problems. But many other, non-health, crises involve you charging around with a thousand things to do, and as many more on your mind. Under those circumstances, energy can indeed become limited: what do you do then?

The first thing to consider is 'In what way is it limited?' Sometimes, a person feels all the time that they have less energy, even when fully rested (a common pattern in depression). For others, it's stamina that's affected; you feel as energetic as ever when well rested, but you tire much more easily than usual once you start doing things. Another possibility is that it takes much longer to recover your energy after exertion than normal. Each of these patterns (and combinations of them) could have different impacts on activity. So, if the problem is mainly one of slow recovery, planning long gaps between tiring activities will help. If your problem is tiring too quickly, you need to pace the activity by doing it more slowly, for shorter periods, or doing just part of it at a time with recovery periods between (this tends to work best if you stop *before* you get utterly exhausted). If you have an overall lack of energy, then it may be a question of prioritising things, working out what it's worth using your limited energy on, and what it's not. You might think of it as energy budgeting, like financial budgeting.[47] And just as with money, if you have less energy to spend, you need to be even more careful how you spend it, working out what are the essentials, trying to save some for 'treats' as well as the necessities, and finding any way you can of making savings (e.g. how important is it to do *all* the ironing?).

Another characteristic of crises is that we often can't control everything about what happens when. However, where we do have choices about when to schedule meetings, tackle paperwork, talk to the family or whatever, it might be worth taking care not to put them one after another if you're going to be exhausted halfway through; you could find yourself handling them much less well than usual.

As a final thought, people sometimes talk about 'emotional energy' in much the same way as physical energy; so they have limited capacity (or stamina, or ability to recover) for dealing with stressful or upsetting events. Even though emotions don't actually work in the same way as muscles, it can still be a useful way of looking at things if it means you are able to better cope with, and take control of, stressful circumstances.

Anil has decided to sit down and force a conversation with Sarah about the question of starting a family, knowing that it will most likely turn into an emotional confrontation about the future of their whole relationship. He's dreading that conversation, but can't stand the uncertainty any longer. Having decided that this Friday evening would be the right time to do it, he now learns that he will be spending most of Friday leading a team making a vital presentation to a potential customer. Past experience tells him that this leaves him edgy and exhausted; not the right state of mind to start one of the most delicate and important conversations of the entire relationship – that will have to wait until Saturday night.

## Key points

- Crises don't happen in a vacuum; the rest of life keeps happening around them. It can be helpful to maintain some normality, but that may require effort.
- How one person thinks others should treat them can be very different to the next person. So, as your friends cannot mind-read, they are bound to get it wrong some of the time. Don't just get angry at them, try to tell them what you need.
- If nervous of what others will ask about your situation, take control of what you say and how you say it. Work it out and practise in advance if necessary.
- Carrying on working as a crisis approaches can bring advantages and disadvantages. If you have been off work, try for a phased return but beware of others' (and your own) expectations.
- Personal relationships matter, and are likely to change (possibly permanently) due to the crisis. It may take extra effort to keep them functioning, or the ability to let some friendships go, while trying to maintain others.
- Disasters hit whole families, not just the individual.
- Name the problem correctly; often it is the crisis (cancer, redundancy, etc.) and not the person or the remedy that is the source of difficulty – don't confuse the two.

- It's right to want to look after the people we love, but beware of 'mutual protection', where hiding things from each other actually makes it harder to cope.
- Someone with genuine concerns won't be helped in the long term by those around them being relentlessly positive; people need to be allowed occasionally to feel bad, and be sympathised with rather than reassured or offered advice.
- Pay particular regard to the needs of children caught up in crises; stay alert to their understanding of the situation, how they are acting towards you, whether they are maintaining their usual activities and friendships and who is available to support them.
- Hobbies and leisure may seem trivial at a time like this, but may meet important personal needs, improve quality of life, and so help you cope.
- Energy can be a limiting factor, and needs to be budgeted carefully (i.e. spend it wisely, try to make savings where you can and try to save some for pleasant treats); however, underactivity can actually make matters worse.

# 7

# Thinking ahead

## Preparing for afterwards

> Depend upon it, sir, when a man knows he is to be hanged
> in a fortnight, it concentrates his mind wonderfully.
>
> Samuel Johnson

As this well-known quotation suggests, knowing that catastrophe is looming tends to keep the mind focused on it (though some people will react in the opposite way, thinking of anything *but* the disaster).

We've already encountered some of the downsides of this kind of focus (if a person becomes obsessed). But here's another: by concentrating on the event itself, we can neglect to give enough thought to what comes afterward. That's not simply a mistake that stressed individuals make; whole organisations can be guilty of the same thing. Many people regard the planning of certain recent wars to have been fatally flawed by giving insufficient thought to what came after the initial battles.

How does this apply to facing catastrophe? Well, even when the separation has happened, the court case taken place (with imprisonment, perhaps), the factory has closed and the house repossessed, there will still be an afterwards, of attempting to live with the consequences of the disaster. Even if you will not survive the disaster, there will still be an aftermath for those who are close to you.

As it becomes clearer to Helen that her death will come sooner rather than later, there are some things that she finds almost too painful to contemplate. The first and biggest of these is how her children will be affected by her death, and how they'll cope without her. She'd give anything to be able to make the future more bearable for them.

One of the principles throughout this book has been that *'just because you can't prevent a disaster doesn't mean there's nothing you can do'*. That applies to aftermaths too; of course you wish the disaster wouldn't happen, but just because it will doesn't mean you give up on the future.

Indeed, this is one of the stronger arguments for knowing that something bad and unavoidable is about to happen because, while ignorance may sound like bliss to some people, it actually robs you of the chance to prepare. Knowing the storm is coming might give you the chance to stock up on water and candles to get through the disruption after it has passed.

So what examples of preparation can we give?

### Doing your homework

Life is shot through with uncertainty, and we never ever know for sure what's going to happen next. However, that's no reason for giving up and saying 'que sera, sera' ('what will be, will be'). By thinking ahead, and doing a little bit of research, we may be able to get an idea of some of the possible ways the future might go.

I often find myself talking to patients and their families about this type of thing, using a process of 'pinning down the extremes'. Although the future of the illness may be uncertain, we can probably isolate the worst plausible outcome (e.g. dying within the next couple of months), the best likely outcome (still being alive five years from now), and a couple of options in between. We can recognise that we don't know which (if any) of these will actually come to pass, but we can think through what sensible courses of action are needed in each case. Although this is another cancer example, the same process is clearly applicable to other crises.

So while there may well be more than one possibility, if we can have some idea of how we would react to each of those possibilities, then there are several benefits:

- We are less likely to be caught unawares at a stage when our energy or problem-solving abilities may be at a low ebb (having gone through the catastrophe).
- We are less likely to end up feeling helpless, or freezing in the face of difficulty, so maintaining a healthier sense of control. It also seems that feeling helpless in a crisis increases the risks of developing post-traumatic stress disorder.[48]
- We can 'anticipate regrets'. This means thinking through what we might end up regretting doing, or not doing now that will make a difference later, but will be too late if we wait.

Although her friends think it pointless, there's something Debbie wants to do before the mill closes; she brings her daughter Beccy in one day to show her round. She tells her:

Take a good look at this. There used to be dozens of these mills in this town alone; now there's one, and next month there'll be none. And it's the same all over the country. You'll never get to see another of these for real, so I wanted to show you what life was like for my generation, and every generation of women round here for over a hundred years. Don't forget it.

And though her daughter doesn't get it right now, years later she is putting together the family history, and she's glad she saw the mill with her own eyes.

At the same time, it's important not to let yourself be ruled by anticipatory regret, because it can lead you into unwise decisions. For instance, it's part of the basic psychology of selling things to people to make them think that, even though they didn't really intend to buy that new pair of shoes, digital camera, or sofa, they'll really regret it later if they miss out on this once-in-a-lifetime sale offer.[49]

## Planning activities

If you knew you were going to hospital for painful surgery with slow recovery, you wouldn't plan a skiing holiday for the following week. Similarly, if you know you're going to have a nightmare time at work, you wouldn't (or shouldn't!) plan the next weekend to be the time you confront some major family problem – as Anil demonstrated in Chapter 6.

With the sort of major life events we're considering in this book, it's all the more important to avoid as far as possible other stressful activities. Now of course they sometimes come along all by themselves without our having any control over them, but some can at least be anticipated. Maybe they can be avoided, or put off until later, or perhaps they can be dealt with earlier – so by getting them out of the way now, there's so much less chance of them becoming urgent when things are in a bad way after a catastrophe.

> Peter, being a thorough kind of man, programs his computer to pop up reminders of things when they need doing – renewing car insurance, filing tax returns and so on. A few weeks before his court case, an automatic reminder comes up to start thinking about writing the annual report for the scout troop AGM in two months' time. In a way, that seems the least of his worries, especially as he might be in prison then; yet he can't face the idea of sending a letter from jail explaining why there's no report. So he decides he'd better settle down and get the thing written now.

## Sorting the practicalities

In palliative care, the phrase 'putting your affairs in order' crops up quite often; people seem to find that easier than talking about making a will, or sorting out the finances (Where are the bank books? Will your surviving partner be able to access cash from your joint account after you've died? Can they afford your funeral?) and so on. The benefits are obvious, but it can take extraordinary resolve to get on and do it.

Most of the time Helen is coping with her advancing cancer, and not dwelling too much on what the future holds, but sometimes it all gets too much and she breaks down; usually that's with her close friend and chemotherapy buddy Zoë. One day she's tearfully describing her thoughts about whether her family would ever be able to cope practically, let alone emotionally, after she's gone. Zoë admits to the same thoughts, especially as she's a single parent relying on her sister to care for her baby if she doesn't survive. But she says that she just keeps reminding herself that she's done what she can; there's a single box file on her bookshelf that holds an updated will, clear statement of what she wants for her own funeral and for her daughter's upbringing, list of all bank accounts, credit cards and insurance policies, and a – slightly tearstained – letter to be given to her daughter on her eighteenth birthday if Zoë isn't around to give it herself.

Helen is a bit surprised; she says she's always seen Zoë as optimistic, and keen to fight the cancer and win. Zoë explains that she is those things; she doesn't see making these preparations as morbid or defeatist. On the contrary, it's taken a weight off her shoulders, as she doesn't have any nagging worries about those issues any more – if anything, it's freed her up mentally to carry on the fight. And if Helen wants to do the same, but Keith would be unable to cope, then Zoë will gladly help her do it.

It makes a big difference whether you're likely to be around after the crisis to help sort matters out; even if you will be, it may be worth getting things lined up as far as possible beforehand, as you may not be in the best mental state in the immediate aftermath.

But, like Helen, you may be facing the possibility of not being there after the crisis – whether that's due to death, long imprisonment, relationship breakdown, or permanent removal overseas. In which case gritting your teeth and thinking through the practicalities (however upsetting that is) becomes essential. It particularly matters for family and close friends, and offers you a way of giving them some element of the support they're about to lose.

---

**Try this now:**

Think about your impending crisis. Make a list of the possible consequences afterwards. Now make a list of any practical steps you can take now to make those things more manageable later. For some (maybe most) there might not be any you can think of right now, but there should be some, however small. The very act of doing this will make it more likely that, if an opportunity to prepare for afterwards does occur, you'll spot it and take it.

---

It tends to work best if the key individuals know and are involved in making the arrangements, but sometimes that's a hard thing for them to do. No matter how realistic they are inside their own heads, they may feel the need to be unrelentingly positive when talking to you. It is also possible that they are fearful of the emotional content of such practical discussions; I've certainly known cases where it was only by doing the apparently pragmatic business of sorting out finances that a couple were for the first time able to acknowledge how sad and scared they both were. Yet, your partner may just never be able to get to that point, and so you simply do the best you can by yourself. Do try to make sure, though, that *someone* knows the work has been done, where the documents are, and that there aren't any out-of-date versions of wills left around to confuse people.

There's another aspect to preparing the family for your absence, and that's communication. Children, in particular, can end up in a difficult situation, not only hurting from their own loss, but also seeing the remaining parent struggling – and for some children, that will lead them to keep quiet about their own thoughts and emotions out of a desire to protect their parent. In Chapter 6 we looked at ways to approach this by finding other avenues of support or channels of communication – perhaps that's something else that becomes doubly important to fix up in advance if you're anticipating not being around much longer.

## Key points

- Don't forget to prepare as best you can for the aftermath of the disaster; if you do, you may a prevent a bad situation from ending up much worse.
- Do your homework, and if the aftermath is uncertain, try to pin down the extremes of best case and worst case, and a couple of possibilities in between.
- Once you have an idea of the spread of possibilities, you can make conditional plans (if 'a' happens then I'll . . ., if 'b' happens then I'll . . .), but be prepared to amend them (or fine-tune them) as you go along.
- Look at what other events are due to happen after your disaster – decide whether they can be dealt with in advance, can be put off until later or not done at all.
- Anticipate regrets, but don't be ruled by them.
- Sort out practicalities for afterwards, including for 'worst case' possibilities. Don't view that as morbid or defeatist, but see it as taking another weight off your shoulders.
- Try to involve others in planning the aftermath. If you can't, make sure there are some written records of your arrangements and preferences if you're not going to be around, and see to it that someone knows they exist and where they are.

# 8

# Riding the storm

## Dealing with the emotions

Most of this book has been about preparing for a crisis. And when the storm finally hits – your partner walks out, the factory closes, you're sent to prison, the person you love dies – then the actions will probably be specific to that particular situation.

But there's one aspect in common between these situations (and, indeed, to many other points in this particular journey): having to deal with strong emotions. It is to this aspect we turn now.

There are whole books about what an emotion actually is. For our purpose, we can think of emotions as strong feelings such as happiness, sadness, anger and others listed below, which may be accompanied by physical changes (e.g. changes in heart rate, or butterflies in the stomach) and may lead to people behaving in a particular way (e.g. anger leading to aggression, sadness leading to withdrawal and crying). Such emotions can well up in us seemingly at any time, but more often than not (and some would argue almost always) they show up alongside some *cognitive* event – a thought, a memory, a mental image or a belief.[50]

Sometimes an emotion is experienced too intensely and/ or too continuously, and that itself becomes a problem. And whether faced with a crisis or not, for all too many people 'normal' sadness (as a reaction to things going badly) can become depression with some or all of its other components (loss of energy, reduced sex-drive, early wakening, hopelessness about the future, inability to experience pleasure). It can be the same if 'normal' anxiety in response to threats becomes a state of constant worry, or the person starts to suffer panic attacks or develops a phobia of people or places. Similar things can be said for all emotions – mostly they're part of a healthy response to life, but there are times when those emotions become problems in themselves (in the jargon, they become 'pathological'). That's generally a time for seeking professional help – possibly via your family doctor in the first instance, or directly consulting a mental health professional, though there are plenty of self-help books relating to all the emotional disorders. Guidance on finding further help is at the back of this book.

But even when we're 'just' talking about appropriate sadness (rather than outright depression), or understandable worry, those emotions can be distressing, intrusive and troublesome, so it's worth looking at ways of dealing with them.

Given that we're dealing with extreme circumstances in this book, it's understandable that emotions can be triggered strongly, and that's probably inevitable. There are some schools of thought that say we *need* to experience these emotions, as suppressing them may store up psychological difficulties for the future. Whether that's true or not, for most of us the emotions will happen anyway, so we need to be clear about what we mean by 'dealing with' them. It's not squashing them down,[51] it's not making them vanish. Rather, it's about trying to reduce any additional damage and suffering they may cause, trying not to let them take over our behaviour entirely, and turning down their intensity when they're getting too much.

Although our emotional responses are shaped by the situation we find ourselves in, the basic range of emotions is the same whether we're facing imminent death, a dentist's appointment or a cliff-hanger in a thriller; the intensity will differ, the nuances will vary and we may use slightly different labels ('dread', 'apprehension', 'tension'), but we are still basically talking about flavours of 'fear'. I sometimes talk about there being a 'cluster' of more or less similar emotional states, so the 'fear' cluster would also include anxiety, panic and worry. Each is different, and those differences can be important, but they have in common a recognisably fear-based feeling. The same can be said for an 'anger' cluster (e.g. frustration, short temper, rage), a 'sadness' cluster (despairing, feeling low, melancholic) and so on. But we must remember that it is absolutely *not* that all states in the cluster are identical; each has its own qualities, is experienced differently, may be triggered by specific things, and some people may be particularly prone to one (anger), and someone else to another (anxiety).

To add to this complexity, emotions are not necessarily experienced singly: a person can be sad and angry, scared and resentful, embarrassed and furious, or pretty well any other combination. And we can't really approach them as 'pure' emotions; they are so tied up with the events provoking them that it becomes impossible to consider a person's grief without looking at the nature of their loss; it's usually a mistake to try to defuse someone's anger without listening to *what* they're angry about.[52]

Having said all that, it's still worthwhile taking a brief look at some of the major emotional states (or perhaps emotional clusters) in order to understand them a little better and mention a couple of things that can help a person bear them, whether during a major crisis or at other times in life. While some will have to be left aside for now – like envy, lust, pride, and one of the most powerful of all, love – there are some that require our closer attention, particularly in relation to coping with major life events. These include sadness, fear, anger, guilt, shame, and (perhaps surprisingly) hope and happiness.

So let's look at these emotions in turn.

**Sadness**

The 'sadness' cluster of emotions tends to be provoked by loss, or by things turning out worse than we might have wanted, whether for ourselves or for others. And that can be loss in the present, in the future or (often) in the past. Given the kinds of situations we are talking about here, there is plenty of scope for potential or actual loss, and things (by definition) not turning out how you would want;

so sadness may be realistic, and may be deserved. And it's important to recognise this, because well-meaning family and friends may try to help by jollying you along, desperately trying to stop you being sad. What often happens then is that you pretend to be happier, but end up feeling more isolated than ever. What you generally need is someone to recognise that you are sad, to acknowledge that it's fair enough to be sad under the circumstances, and not pressure you too much over it.

Yet there comes a limit where prolonged periods of focusing on how sad we feel begins to make matters worse; it actually adds to what was already a difficult situation.[53] So the principle is that we have a right to feel sad, and even to wallow – a bit. Then we have to do things to manage the sadness – not erase it or suppress it (it'll still be there) but not let it take over completely. There are several things that can help.

### *Distraction*

Sadness is partly maintained by the thoughts that are going through our heads – of what's gone wrong, of what we've lost. They may well deserve thinking about, but hours and days of dwelling on the same things just makes matters worse – not least because when we're feeling sad, it gets easier to have negative thoughts and harder to have positive ones. But the tendency to sit or lie thinking about these things means that we are not doing other things, so there is less distraction. Distraction certainly won't make the problems go away, but it gives the mind something else to be occupied with some of the time, and gives the sad thoughts and sad feelings less chance to be in complete control. So the ideal distraction is something that requires thought as well as action; for example, it's easy to mow the lawn and be miles away in our thoughts, possibly negative ones. Something with a mental challenge (being part of a conversation, doing a puzzle or quiz, making a complicated recipe) is far more likely to give a rest from the negative thoughts. Similarly, if a person is tending to lie awake thinking about the troubles, it can be much more useful to have speech radio on rather than music, as speech is more mentally involving, whereas music can easily become 'wallpaper' that's not really noticed, or (depending on the song) can actually make you feel worse.[54]

And be a little wary of relying too much on distraction; the short-term benefits of using it to manage your mood can be lost if you're so busy with distraction that you're no longer doing any of the things that matter in your life. Also, distraction can become an obsession in itself, or it becomes an act of suppressing a thought – likely leading to that thought becoming more intrusive.

### *Activity*

In part, activity is useful for the distraction it provides. But even taking the example of mowing the lawn (not necessarily the most distracting activity), there would seem to be a benefit just in doing something, certainly in contrast to sitting still the whole time. But here lies the problem: low mood saps the will to get on with things, making it more likely that the person ends up simply staying in bed or on the couch. As we've seen before, that gives more scope for the negative thoughts and sadness to take over, making it even less likely that they'll initiate any action, and so on. This is one of the classic 'vicious circles' that can keep a person trapped in an unwanted mood for long periods.[55] For those who have become very low (maybe with the other components of depression) to the point of inactivity, we sometimes have to plan scheduled activity. We divide the day into three segments, and within each segment plan one (brief) activity that will make the person feel more in control (maybe getting a single household chore done) and one that would *normally* bring them pleasure (a short walk, reading a magazine). And that can be a useful technique when whatever disaster you're facing makes you feel like giving up.[56]

Just as Anil had feared, Sarah did finally leave him, and for the next few weeks, he went to pieces. True, he managed to get himself to work most days, but at the flat he simply lay around with the TV on but not watching it, increasingly surrounded by empty pizza boxes. The sight of the rooms that he normally liked to keep neat and clean becoming messy and unhygienic further strengthened his sense of worthlessness and loss. It took his sister to speak firmly to him, and suggest that one evening he put an hour into tidying and cleaning the living room, and afterwards come out to the pub for a drink. Then maybe the next day he could sort out the bathroom and a little later watch a favourite DVD. None of it was easy, and all the activities were done grudgingly, but within a few days life was getting a little more back to normal. Although the sadness was still there, he didn't feel quite such a slob.

### *Positive events*

One of the other ways that low moods (and indeed depression) keep themselves going is by the lack of positive events. The loss of initiative described above combines with the fact that it gets harder to feel happy. This means that not only do people often stop doing the boring-but-necessary things (like housework), but also they stop doing things that would normally bring pleasure, so there's less to challenge the negative feeling, making the person sadder, making them less likely to do positive things, making them feel more down . . . a similar vicious circle to the last one. That's why the scheduled activity technique we've just looked at includes activities that would normally bring pleasure. And the 'would normally bring' description is crucial here, because there's a paradox. We normally do leisure and pleasure type things because they make us feel happy, we enjoy them; if we didn't enjoy them, we wouldn't do them. But when we're very low, we often find it difficult to experience happiness, enjoyment, or fun,[57] so asking the low or depressed person to do fun things seems self-defeating – why should they bother? But, even if we are just 'going through the motions', doing those things that would normally bring pleasure seems to gradually increase the ability to experience pleasure, and soon they are actually capable of bringing happiness again (often very soon). So the essential principle is to do those activities because they will gradually make you feel better rather than because they bring pleasure straight away. In a way, it's treating them as medicine to be swallowed, even if we have to hold our nose while doing it.

## Exercise

I always feel a bit mean pointing this out to my patients. After all someone's had a really rough time finding out they've got cancer, coming through a programme of, say, chemotherapy and now, though physically stronger, have finally become overwhelmed psychologically. Someone refers them to the clinical psychologist to help them and he starts encouraging them to get more exercise! Of course people need some self-care, maybe a bit of pampering, but the evidence is fairly clear that for both the low mood and the loss of energy that people often experience in this situation, one of the very best things they can do is to start taking regular exercise. Nothing too extreme, and (of course) in line with their doctor's recommendation. It would appear that, as well as constituting regular activity, and providing some degree of distraction and a sense of achievement, there is some direct mood-altering effect of exercise, via one or more hormones secreted during exercise.[58] And if it can be a form of exercise you find pleasant, that's yet another reason for it to impact on mood. And more so if there's a social element to it.

## Careful cognitive challenge

This is one of the trickiest ones, because people usually feel they've tried it and failed. Cognitive challenge basically means arguing back against the negative thoughts in your head; this is one of the core elements of cognitive therapy, and a damned sight harder than it sounds. Hard because the part of you that's trying to be so rational and challenging to the negative thought is also the same part (i.e. the mind) that is being influenced by the sadness, and by definition finding it hard to see things straight. Yet the success of cognitive behavioural therapy demonstrates that properly done, and applied to the right 'targets', it can be very successful.[59]

Our problem in the 'facing disaster' situation is that some of the thoughts are hard to argue against. So, while most people can find a possible argument back against thoughts like 'Nobody likes me' and 'Everything I do fails', it can be harder to know what to do about thoughts like 'My wife is going to leave me', 'I'm going to lose the business I've spent my life building up' or 'I'm going to die', especially when they are objectively true. As it turns out, one can still 'do' cognitive therapy with these types of thoughts, but it takes a certain amount of care if it's not going to end up being rather insulting and unrealistic. On a moment-to-moment basis, even in the midst of problems, some of our negative thoughts are indeed inaccurate: '*Everything* will always turn out badly for me' or 'I have achieved *nothing* in my life'. Unchallenged, such thoughts are treated as being true; and if any of us genuinely believed that *everything* would always go wrong, then of course we would feel pretty bad.

---

**Try this now:**

If you've been feeling more down or worried or angry than usual, try keeping a simple thought diary. Every time your mood takes a turn for the worse, note the date and time, which emotion you experienced (sadness, fear, anger and so on) and what was going through your head at the time. That way, after collecting information for a while, you'll begin to recognise your recurring negative thoughts. And once you start to spot them, they begin to lose some of their power over you, as we'll see below.

---

A word of caution here, though. It's very understandable to react to unwanted thoughts and feelings by striving to get rid of them. However, there is a real danger of getting so absorbed in the struggle against them that all the internal arguing and seeking distraction gets in the way of your life just as much as the mood ever did.[60] We'll return to this in Chapter 9, but in the mean time, bear in mind the principle of 'workability': whichever techniques work for you (help you live the kind of life you'd want to) are the ones to keep on with.

## Fear

### *The nature of fear*

Our next emotion cluster is the range of different states that all have an element of fear about them, from the thinking and rumination of 'worry', to the heart-pounding, sweating, trapped sensation of 'panic'. They have in common the anticipation of something bad which may be about to happen (whereas sadness is, as we have seen, often linked to something bad already having happened). To some extent, the precise emotional experience depends on how immediate and how terrible the 'something bad' is: the prospect of visiting the dentist next week is different from being trapped in a crashed car and able to smell both petrol and burning wires. We have to be careful, though, since even here individual differences play a huge part. I once met someone who had stayed calm during (and after) such a car crash, but was thrown into a full-on panic attack by the prospect of phoning the dentist for an appointment. As we've seen so many times before, it is not the event itself which shapes a person's reaction, but rather what it means to them.[61]

The theme of this book has been that, while we all live in an uncertain and risky world, there is something different about situations where really bad things are almost definitely about to happen. And sometimes, that's not obvious to people who aren't in the situation themselves.

Throughout her worsening illness, Helen has tried to be tolerant when other people say tactless or unhelpful things to her. She snapped once, though; she had a meeting with her bank manager to discuss insurance and mortgage matters. He was clearly uncomfortable about having to discuss the fact that she was planning for being dead within the year. 'Of course,' he said, 'we all have to face these things. After all, I could be knocked down by a bus tomorrow.'

Rather than just smiling sweetly (as she normally would), Helen heard herself saying, 'Sure. The difference is that you aren't standing at the bus stop, watching the bus hurtle towards you with your name on the front, with the only doubt being exactly *when* it's going to hit you.'

The threats we are addressing here actually deserve some respect for being major, inevitable and imminent. And any discussion of how to cope with the fear they cause needs to take account of that. These are not things easily reasoned away. I go back to the final part of the previous section on sad thoughts: there may be aspects of the worrying thoughts that can be open to careful cognitive challenge, for example where a person is not just thinking 'This is going to be really bad, and will hit my family hard', but is telling herself 'This is the end of everything for me – I have no future, and my children will never be happy again'. There is a difference, but a person sometimes needs help to see it, and that help has to be careful and tactful. And sometimes, we aren't able to take it from our nearest and dearest; we'll only listen to a stranger, and then we will probably only accept the modified thought if we've reached it by ourselves rather than being told it. In cognitive behavioural therapy this is called 'guided discovery', and is a central part of the approach.[62]

Because many worries in these situations are 'fair enough' given what is about to happen, it's reasonable to ask whether the anxiety is itself inevitable, and any attempt to control it foolish, or at worst a dangerous exercise in encouraging denial of the problem. There are two things to say about that: it's generally best if attempts to cope don't involve lying to yourself (though we all do that sometimes), and yes, some anxiety may be unavoidable; but if that anxiety escalates to the point of making someone 'freeze', incapable of taking appropriate action, or developing some kind of panic that becomes a problem in itself, then that needs handling. There's a slightly odd logic I sometimes hear, that because significant sadness, fear or anger are understandable consequences of personal crises, we shouldn't try to do anything about them. Yet pain is an understandable consequence of many forms of cancer, but no one suggests that we shouldn't try to limit or manage that.

So if fear has such unpleasant and disabling effects, and can make a difficult situation even harder, why do we all have it? And 'we' doesn't just mean adult humans; it's one of the earliest emotions we see in children. What's more, if we see a startled or cornered animal we might not be able to know exactly how it is feeling, but it would seem perverse not to describe the reaction of an ape, dog or bird as fear (though we might be less confident when it comes to, say, an ant or a sea-slug). That kind of tendency across different species suggests something that, in evolutionary terms, it either had a major survival advantage for our ancestors, or was a side-effect of something that did.

The standard explanation of why fear is so universal is linked to something called the 'fight or flight' reaction; it's an idea that's been around for nearly 100 years, and is perhaps a little oversimplified,[63] but it is still useful. It is typically illustrated by considering a hypothetical caveman. Imagine (the story goes) someone going in to a cave to search for food or shelter. At some point he notices a shadow which may well be a sabre-tooth tiger. Within the next few moments he might have to fight for his life, or flee for his life (hence 'fight or flight'). What might increase his chances of survival? Well, physical changes like tensing up the major muscle groups (to struggle or run), giving them a good supply of fuel by increasing blood flow through them (increasing heart rate and blood pressure), and making sure that blood has plenty of oxygen in it (by increasing the breathing rate). Of course, there will be other consequences of these changes – for instance muscles kept tense get hot, so sweat may be needed to control their temperature. The rise in blood pressure may lead to sensations of dizziness or tingling. But these changes are not all physical. He'll also be helped by becoming very alert, reacting quickly to any new movement or sound, treating it as if it might be another tiger – which is to say that he'll startle easily, and will start to see danger everywhere – because it's safer to over-react than to under-react. He'll also be helped by some very basic rules of what to do next:

1 Get out of there.
2 Don't go back.
3 If you do have to go back, get into this state of readiness beforehand, just in case.
4 In general, try to avoid places or situations that make you feel like this, because they're likely to be dangerous.

So that is, in essence, the fight or flight reaction, and we all have it in us, as (it is argued) we're all the descendants of the creatures who had it – because those without it got eaten.

What's more, some argue, it's actually a fairly 'dumb' system: it gets triggered by a perceived threat and then fires up without much reference to the exact nature of the threat. And that's probably OK when most of the threats in your environment are things that are going to eat you or drop on you; indeed, it's still pretty useful if you're chased by a vicious dog or discover burglars in your house. But the problem for modern humans is that most of the threats we face are not ones best sorted out by punching someone or 'legging it'; they're things like facing a job interview, finding we can't pay a bill or speaking in public. And those are things that are actually made worse by being tense, heart-pounding, sweating, jittery, and having a desperate urge to hit someone or run away and never return. But because 'fight or flight' doesn't distinguish between *types* of imminent threat, exactly those things can happen. And if you add in those behavioural rules (avoid that situation in future, and if you have to go there, start your fight or flight reaction early) you have a recipe for building up a phobia for such places or activities. Indeed, that seems to be how many phobias work. And if it's not a full-blown phobia, you can still find that you've allowed your 'avoidance of anxiety' to choose your actions, rather than deciding for yourself what matters most to you.[64]

Not every threat sets off the full fight or flight response, but (the argument goes) even the more toned-down forms of anxiety we frequently experience probably have their roots in its original survival advantage. There may be fewer overwhelming physical symptoms, but some increase in arousal (basically, how 'worked up' you are) is a common part of our experience of anxiety.

And the (presumably) more uniquely human trait of 'worry', with its repetitive going-over of troubling thoughts, can be seen as another form of that shift of attention towards possible threat that we saw in our caveman. One line of reasoning about how humans came to evolve more complex brains and minds than other animals is that there is a survival benefit to being able to think in abstract terms. So rather than thinking 'Where are there berries?', thinking 'How can I make berries grow close to the village?' And (with direct relevance to our topic here) rather than thinking 'There's a tiger attacking us . . . again', thinking 'How are the tigers getting into the valley? How can we stop them getting this close to the huts?' So the threat is not simply dealt with at the moment it is happening, but is being considered and (let's hope) solved within the person's head, possibly over a period of time greater than the length of a tiger attack. Again, the survival benefits would be clear, but as with most things, there would be a price to pay. Rather than just having problems with tigers on the occasion they attack, there is longer-term tiger-related stress going on during the hours of thinking about tiger attacks and possible defences. And that's where we link to our contemporary examples, as time spent thinking in advance about, say, an upcoming court trial might help the person build better arguments and be more fully prepared, but the cost might be months of worry and sleeplessness concerning a two-day court case (I had a colleague who sometimes used to appear in court as part of her job; she used to measure how worrying an upcoming case was by how many toilet rolls she got through in the week before it).

These accounts of the 'why' and the 'how' of fear, anxiety and worry tend to make a lot of sense to people currently experiencing difficulties in this area, and it can help plan treatments for those people who can no longer face that trip to the supermarket, or can't sleep for going over and over the same worries. But as neat and as useful as these explanations are, there a few cautions to bear in mind. Stories of the evolutionary reason for things are bound to be speculative (as neither you nor I were there at the time), and with the inevitable lack of direct evidence it can be tempting to believe that any neat and plausible explanation must definitely be true (in another reference to Kipling, some refer to evolutionary explanations of behaviour as 'Just So Stories').[65] There are also many differences in reactions to threat between species, between sexes and between individuals, many no doubt due to the effects of all the factors that the caveman story leaves out, such as differences in past experience, in personality and in physical constitution.

I do believe, though, that managing anxiety in the presence of genuine threat is more feasible if we acknowledge that anxiety is here for a reason, and our goal cannot be to eliminate every trace of it, but rather to keep its impact within reasonable limits, and – as best we can – make sure we choose the actions that we think matter, rather than just those that our caveman anxiety wants us to choose.

So now we've accepted how and why worry is there, how *do* we manage its impact? Well, the first (and maybe most important) part is remembering what we've just learnt: that worries are mental events (thoughts, pictures, feelings) that are related to bad things, but they are not the bad things themselves. Being in court may be scary, but at 3 a.m. a month beforehand, it's not being in court that is upsetting you – because you're not there! It is a *thought* about a court case, a mental event happening purely within your own head. If you're choosing to think about it, in order to plan your defence or whatever, then fine: go ahead. But most of the time you're not choosing; the thought has simply got stuck in there and is occupying your attention.[66]

Now, a court case is a big event, with lots of people, stress and the possibility of a bad outcome. A thought is a set of tiny electrical impulses taking place in your brain. And no matter how important and real the thing that the thoughts refer to actually is, at the moment you are worrying, it is not the bad thing (here, the trial), but the *thought* of the thing which is troubling you. So the key distinction to make is the thing, versus the thought of the thing. I was trying to explain this once to my younger son, who was worrying about something one night, and I ended up saying, 'Worrying about there being a mad bear in your bedroom would be bad. But it's not the same as there actually *being* a mad bear in your room.'

The very act of noticing that you're having a thought about $x$ – sometimes called 'defusion' – helps give you a little mental distance from it.

None of this is belittling the real problems a person is facing and, as we've already seen, it's understandable that we end up spending time thinking over them. But when something has been worrying you for a while, what are the chances that another five minutes of thinking about it, or ten, or an hour, will actually solve it? Unlikely. At that moment, your problem is not the court case, the marital breakdown, the terminal illness; it's that you're spending time fruitlessly worrying about it.

So what should we do?

### Strategies for dealing with worry

#### Disengaging from worry

Our first strategy suggests that, rather than carrying on with the worry and trying to solve the problem, we can try to:

1 **Notice** that we have started worrying, and what we are worrying about.
2 **Choose** not to get involved in the thought, because we're not likely to solve it right now.

3 **Remind** ourselves that, at this precise moment, it is a thought that is troubling us, not the thing that the thought is about.

4 **Redirect** the attention somewhere else; people typically try to 'think about something nice' – a daydream, or a happy memory.

But that sometimes won't work, so you might go for distraction; external distraction would be reading a book, listening to the radio, doing a crossword puzzle. But if they're not practical, there are internal distraction tasks:

- Counting backwards in threes from 200 (certainly a challenge for me!).
- Trying to remember in as much detail as possible a route you've gone down many times.
- Trying to recall a favourite movie scene by scene.
- In your head, describing something you can see (e.g. a door) in such complete detail that someone listening to the description would be able to picture it perfectly.

The idea is that if your mind is absorbed in something demanding like these activities there won't be as much room left for the worries to occupy. Now clearly, you can't just spend the rest of your life filling your head up with these other activities – that would be as bad as the worries themselves; but what we're actually aiming for is a brief period of occupying the mind in order to break the worry's hold on your attention. That leaves the question of what happens when your mind wanders back to the worry. When we discuss mindfulness in Chapter 9, we'll deal with that.

*Worry Time*

Given that we've already acknowledged that some of these worries are actually important, it may not be feasible (or even sensible) to block them out permanently. That's where we get to Worry Time. Rather than spend fruitless hours fretting over the worries, allocate a period of perhaps 15 minutes at a fixed time each day, when you will sit down with a pad of paper and pen, and consciously think over the problems. Try to think of any new angles or possibilities, and whatever you come up with, make sure it gets written down. If you don't come up with anything new, so be it. At the end of the period, put the pad and pen away and go and do something distracting (some people plan Worry Time to be the 15 minutes before a favourite TV or radio programme) so that you don't continue to dwell on the problem. When worries come at other times, you can put off considering them until the next Worry Time, confident that you're not simply ignoring the problems, because you will be returning to them in less than 24 hours. And you must; for this isn't some con-trick where you then 'forget' to have Worry Time, because we've already agreed that these matters are important enough to deserve some serious consideration but not constant, unhelpful chewing over. Also, by keeping the notepad and pen close to hand, if there is something new and important that comes to you at 3 a.m. you can write it down ready for the next Worry Time. That way you don't have to delve into it there and then, or carry it in your head, but you'll still know that you're not going to forget it.[67]

Worry Time can work well, not only as a way of stopping the intrusive thoughts, but also because a planned 15 minutes of consideration is far more likely to be productive than endless, stress-tinged rumination.

Sometimes, the worries are actually collections of different related thoughts – maybe all about your father, or about money problems. To stop yourself getting too tangled up in them, when they occur you could picture them as an old-fashioned box file labelled 'Dad' or 'Money Worries'; they can be recognised and put aside as a group, but at times (e.g. Worry Time) you can choose to 'open' that box file and sort through the papers within, then close it again. And the next time the worries creep in, just see in your mind's eye the box file that you'll put aside until next Worry Time.

*Relaxation*

One of the obvious ways that people try to cope with anxiety is to relax; after all, stress and arousal are at the core of any fear-type response, so trying to unwind is the natural response to getting wound up. In my experience, it tends not to be enough by itself when there are intrusive thoughts nagging away in the background; but if you're not troubled by them, or alternatively you've learned to deal with them using the techniques above, it can make a big difference.

Relaxation is a very personal business; you might find decorating relaxing, but it drives me to distraction. I'll happily chill out to 1970s Prog Rock, which makes my wife want to throw the hi-fi through the window. So the key thing is to know what relaxes you (and try not to stress out your nearest and dearest in the process). There seem to be different ingredients in what makes an activity relaxing for people. An obvious one is something that reduces tension and arousal – maybe a warm bath and gentle music. That also brings in the element of pampering oneself – consciously choosing not to be busy, or achieving things; some say it's spending time just *being* rather than *doing*.[68]

But there are other activities that people find relaxing which aren't necessarily physically calming – walking, sport, gardening, do-it-yourself and so on. This type of activity seems to relax by absorbing the mind in something far different from the pressures and worries of daily life. Of course, you can be walking in the hills and fretting about your relationship, or digging the vegetable plot and fantasising about burying your boss there. But, when done as relaxation, these activities engage the mind in the present moment – not the past or the future, or what's going on elsewhere.

There had been times in Anil's relationship when his weekly sessions of five-a-side football had caused a little friction with Sarah. The fact that Tuesday evenings (and some Sunday mornings) were spoken for sometimes felt like an imposition on their time together. And it was hard for Anil to explain why he felt more stressed if sessions were cancelled.

But during the relationship break-up, he realised why the games had become even more essential to him. For that hour or so, his mind was entirely focused on where the ball was going, who it was going to be passed to next, where gaps in the field were emerging, not making a mistake with timing his passes, trying to keep breathing despite feeling like passing out. The rest of his time might be absorbed with thoughts of what had gone wrong in the past, of where Sarah was right now (and who she was with), and of what a future without her would be like, but while he was playing, the only things on his mind were those that were happening right now, right here. And that gave him a kind of mental release that, for all the sweating and breathlessness, was the most relaxing state of mind he could achieve.

This kind of utter mental absorption is sometimes called 'flow';[69] I first heard the term when rock-climbers were discussing the peculiar attractions of their sport, but it's not just for life-threatening pastimes. I used to be involved in a rather unusual weekend course for senior cancer doctors and nurses, taking them out of their hectic clinical settings and spending time using the arts (listening to music, talking about favourite pictures and so on) to work on their ability to see the world through others' eyes (an essential skill for supporting people with a life-threatening illness, but not in the past a feature of a traditional medical education).[70] At one point, they would spend a couple of hours trying out a simple kind of print-making. After the first few minutes of (usually relaxed) chatter and joking, the room would get progressively quieter and quieter as people became more absorbed in the print they were making. Afterwards, people would comment that their mind was totally involved in the activity, that they barely thought of anything else and they felt utterly calm. The contrast with their working life and indeed the family life they were trying to juggle with it couldn't have been more marked. One or two of them went on to do evening art classes, and said it really helped their stress management.

So, in looking for relaxation, inactivity and pampering may play a part, but they aren't the only options.

In addition to the kinds of activities that bring relaxation as a very desirable side-effect, there are also ones that are mainly or entirely aimed at relaxation. These include yoga, Tai Chi, complementary therapies, visualisation, hypnosis and meditation.

### Yoga

Obviously, yoga also aims for physical benefits, but is very likely to have a component of mental calming – either due to focusing on physical sensation during stretches and positions, or as a separate part of the session using techniques like visualisation (see below).

### Tai Chi

Tai Chi (and 'cousins' to it like Qi Gong) has some similarities to yoga; it comprises a set of movements which one can take a lifetime perfecting (or rather, improving, as 'perfection' of movement might not be an achievable goal). Again, the mental focus upon all the many components of the set bodily movements can give that absorption and flow we've been talking about.[71]

### Complementary therapies

Complementary therapies prove very popular and useful for people affected by serious illness. A few of the therapies aim for direct physical benefit (e.g. pain relief, reduced nausea) with differing degrees of evidence. But most aim for relaxation and stress management, and can do so very effectively. The list is almost endless, but massage and aromatherapy are two of the most widely available and appreciated. The next couple of techniques are often classed as complementary therapy, but have some specific aspects that I'd like to address individually.

Visualisation

Visualisation can be used alone, as a core component of hypnosis (see below) or sometimes used as part of a yoga session (and occasionally at the end of sports training sessions). It involves creating a vivid mental image, often including senses other than vision – sounds, touch, smell – and spending some period of time dwelling in it.[72] Two of the standard ones are

- lying on a beach, sunshine, gentle breeze, sounds of the sea, swaying palm trees and so on, or (for people like me who are allergic to beach holidays)
- a woodland with paths, cool streams, sound of wind through leaves, dappled sunshine, birdsong.

There seem to be several active ingredients here: time spent not doing anything else, settings that are – for many people – associated with calmness and tranquillity, the fact that, being personal and internal creations, they cannot be disrupted or spoiled by irritating things (like mosquitoes, sunburn or mobile phones) that might exist in the real version, and finally the very fact that creating a detailed 'virtual reality' absorbs a lot of mental capacity, so it achieves the goal of distraction we discussed earlier.

Hypnosis

Hypnosis can be used in many ways – as a stage entertainment, as an approach to stopping smoking or overeating, as part of a psychological treatment package for addressing entrenched problems, or 'just' for relaxation. Inducing a hypnotic state often involves focusing the attention in a particular way, and suggesting that certain sensations are being experienced. Much of the skill that someone is learning in hypnosis (as the client, not the therapist) is in 'deepening' the state, so that the individual is deeply relaxed, but paying attention to the internal world being created rather than the external one. This often involves a detailed and elaborate visualisation which may include moving towards (often downwards into) a personal 'safe place'. This could be the kind of beach or wood scene discussed under visualisation, or almost anything that is right for that particular individual. Time spent in that place could simply be relaxing – possibly boosted by the increased vividness and sense of reality given by a hypnotic state – but can also entail other activities which can symbolically give the person a greater sense of strength, control, confidence and so on. An example might be drinking from a stream where the water fills you with a sense of self-confidence. So hypnosis, properly done, can not only provide deep relaxation for someone who is in the state, but also make them feel more confident about facing life after the session is over.[73]

## Meditation

Meditation has a significant overlap with yoga, and indeed with much of what I have been saying about keeping the mind in the present (rather than the past, the future, or what's going on elsewhere). For while many people's image of meditation might be of someone sitting cross-legged under a tree for hours on end, we could argue that a meditative state is one where the mind is seeking to focus upon one thing, and whenever it wanders is brought back to that thing. And that means that you can meditate on the sensations of a yoga position, on the feelings in your feet and legs while walking, on the flow of a five-a-side football match you are participating in, or the experience of eating a bacon sandwich. And while the roots of meditation as a practice generally lie in eastern traditions such as Buddhism, it's not hard to see that the meditative state is something that exists all by itself, and that people can get into it in a variety of ways, whether or not they have even heard the word 'meditation'.[74] There is one type of meditation that has become so useful in dealing with stress and life events – 'mindfulness' – that I plan to devote a large part of Chapter 9 to it, as it applies to all of the emotional states, so I won't discuss it further here.

Two final points about relaxation in general, and both of them are cautions. First, some people find that suddenly becoming much more relaxed during one of the activities listed above can actually feel uncomfortable or downright unpleasant; occasionally we see relaxation-induced panic,[75] which is fairly self-explanatory. The best solution is a little perseverance to see whether it passes, and if it doesn't then try a different one of the above approaches, maybe one that you don't find so 'deep'.

The second caution is about striving too hard; if you put a lot of effort into trying to relax, that effort itself can stop you relaxing. Better to hold that goal fairly lightly and appreciate feeling a little calmer, rather than beating yourself up for not being more tranquil!

We've spent a long time looking at fear, anxiety and worry, and some of the ways of coping with them. I think, though, that reflects the fact that these are some of the most common and undermining aspects of dealing with crises. But of course, even if anxiety and sadness are two of the commoner emotional reactions, they are very far from the only ones.

## Anger

As with the other emotions we've dealt with here, the term 'anger' covers a whole range of particular states, from mild irritability through to murderous rage. The causes of anger can be many, but are often some perceived threat or challenge, or the need to protect another (the 'lioness' factor), some perceived unfairness or the frustration of being somehow prevented from doing something that mattered to you (a sadly common experience in serious illnesses and injuries).

Alongside these causes we should also remember that anger can sometimes be 'goal-directed', used as a way of achieving something – think of street protests or the tantrums of prima donna celebrities (of either gender). Sometimes that may be completely faked emotion, of course, but more often it is genuine anger which is being more or less consciously harnessed to have an impact on other parties –

whether that is the government of the day or a hotel receptionist who has failed to provide the perfect room.

Another way that anger may not be what it seems is when it acts as a vent for other emotions. The analogy people often use here is that of a volcano: pressure builds up underground, getting greater but staying invisible. At some point, a weak spot will give way (possibly due to some minor last straw), and all the repressed emotion explodes outwards.

During the time he's been preparing for his court case, Peter has become increasingly obsessed with it, and his wife Alice has noticed that he's more and more tense. Having known him so well over the years, she can tell he's suffering inside. Yet any attempts to discuss it are met with a slightly clipped 'I'm fine. Really. Now I have to get on with . . .' Then one evening she hears a commotion from the garage. She finds Peter sitting, sobbing, in the middle of a chaos of tools, paint tins, smashed plant pots, and with his bike wheel a tangled mess of spokes surrounding the hammer that has smashed them. She eventually works out that he was trying to put a tyre back on the wheel after repairing a puncture, and couldn't get it to fit cleanly back on the rim. After trying fairly patiently the first few times, he suddenly found himself throwing the tyre levers across the garage, smashing the wheel with a claw hammer, then turning his attention to everything around him, hitting, throwing and smashing until the fury turned into tears, and he was overwhelmed by how terrible his life was. That night, for the first time, he's able to talk to Alice about how he feels: his fears for what will happen to them all if he's convicted, his anger at how he's been treated by his bank and the police, his despair that all his dreams of success and hard work have come to nothing, and with bankruptcy and a criminal conviction to his name, how he'll never again have the chance to succeed.

And the next morning, he goes back to being his usual self-contained, emotionally repressed self.

It's particularly common for anger to act as a vent for long-term worry and anxiety – that's one of the reasons why parents who have spent hours waiting and worrying about a teenager who is late home will often flip into fury at them as soon as they are back safely. In part, this is because anxiety and anger are physically very similar states.[76]

Our problem is often that the anger gets directed at the wrong people or things – people may be passive towards those who are giving them a hard time, and then lose their temper at their own family and friends. Unfortunately, this can cause problems of its own, with conflict becoming a new source of stress, and people who have previously been supportive rapidly backing off.

And to make matters worse, people are often not aware of just how bad-tempered they're getting, or see it as an automatic consequence of the stressful situation, rather than its having anything to do with them.

So, how are we to deal with this kind of anger? Well, addressing some of the underlying worries that it ends up venting is ideal but that's not always 100 per cent possible. Other helpful strategies include the following:

- Spot when you are getting angry – or listen if others point it out to you. People often experience anger as 'just snapping' or coming without warning. Yet when I get people to keep diaries of episodes of losing their temper, they soon realise that tension has usually been building up for some time beforehand. Learn to spot the situations that consistently begin to wind you up – however major or minor they are. Also, try to learn the warning signs within your body that you're winding up: for some people it could be tension across the back of the neck, or feeling hotter, or noticing your heartbeat increasing. All, of course, are parts of the fight or flight response.
- Identify what you're actually angry about. You may need to wait until you've calmed down to do this. Try to look past the immediate trigger (e.g. the telephone helpline that puts you on hold, your child spilling cereal on the carpet again, or the tyre that won't go back on its rim) and see whether it deserves your anger – it might well

do, since anger can be every bit as reasonable an emotional response to bad events as anxiety or sadness. But don't let your anger towards cancer, the police, or fate become anger against your partner or children.

- Learn some simple calming-down procedures. The old 'counting to ten' trick has a lot to be said for it, but if you learn some sort of basic relaxation practice (e.g. two slow breaths, saying 'calm' inside your head on each out-breath, and making sure your shoulders relax) that can be even more effective.
- If you need to (and you safely can), walk away from the situation rather than allow it to escalate.

Some of these steps will help with controlling immediate anger; others such as dealing with underlying worries and working out what you're actually angry about should help prevent recurrences of it. But another potent way of dealing with the accumulation of anger is to burn it off.[77] Remember in the classic fight or flight response, the body was preparing itself to run away or strike out; in anger as in panic, the body is geared up for explosive action, and constant bottling up can add to the potential for a volcano later. So – within the limits of your health and fitness – try giving your muscles the kind of activity they've geared themselves up for, such as digging the garden, running, cycling, lifting weights, hitting a punchbag. My own favourite is playing squash – the tougher the day I've had, the harder I hit the ball; now as squash players will know, just hitting it harder all the time isn't a good way to win, but it certainly feels good. And you don't have to be able to do these things at the very moment you're most stressed – having a regular outlet of this sort should help with the background build-up of tension.

A couple of warnings, though: beware of any of this working out of anger harming (or scaring) others, and be careful also of driving yourself too hard and inducing anything from a pulled muscle to a heart attack.

A final point to make about anger is this – it's not all bad. While it can be divisive, destructive and energy sapping, it's also true that amazing things can be achieved when anger gets channelled in the right way: healthcare provision improves, laws are changed, tyrants fall. And at the individual level, it can give a person the drive and fire to keep going – so long as you don't let that fire consume you. The broader point here is that emotions aren't truly negative or positive, but are just a natural part of living life; it's when we get lost in them, or act on them unwisely that the problems really start.

When people are talking about emotional distress, then sadness, anxiety and anger are probably the 'big three' that receive most attention. That doesn't mean though that other emotions can't cause difficulties of their own.

## Guilt

Feeling bad about something we've done wrong can be corrosive and hang over a person for the rest of their life; one of the ways that some people's upbringing (by a family, school or religion) scars them for ever is via guilt for something that cannot change. And yet the self-punishment of guilt can also be powerful in shaping ourselves towards better behaviour in the future, becoming part of what some people call a 'moral compass', telling us the right way to go.[78]

A distinction (though a subjective one) is sometimes made between *rational* guilt and *irrational* guilt. So for example if for years you've purposely treated someone badly who doesn't deserve it, then feeling guilty about it might be seen as rational. On the other hand, people can end up feeling terribly guilty for things that no one else sees as being their fault.

> Helen's state is deteriorating, and her palliative care nurse asks her where she would rather spend her final days – at home, in the local hospital or at the hospice (if a bed is available). This makes her very tearful, and unable to discuss it at that appointment. On the following visit, she admits her tears were not because of the prospect of her own death, but because of memories of her mother's terminal illness. Helen's mother had a deep fear

of hospitals, and repeatedly made Helen promise to keep her at home right to the end. As her main carer, Helen took more and more of the burden of nursing care, but persevered in order to meet her promise. Eventually, though, her mother developed more difficult and complicated symptoms which needed constant monitoring and changes from her medical team, so she ended up spending her final days in hospital. And though she died peacefully and in comfort, Helen has always secretly carried a sense of guilt for breaking her promise to keep her mother at home. So when considering her own preferred place of dying, Helen is very clear about not putting any expectations on her partner or daughter, to spare them any risk of the same kind of guilt.

Of course, whether guilt is rational or irrational in a particular case is a subjective judgement, because it deals with our sense of moral rights and wrongs, and they vary a lot. As a rule of thumb, though, one can argue that:

• we should feel guilty only about what we're actually responsible for and
• we're responsible only for those things we have control over (or have chosen).

So the train driver whose train kills someone walking along the track could quite reasonably argue that he or she had no control over the event (given that a train can take over a mile to stop in an emergency), and therefore needn't feel responsible. That doesn't guarantee that the driver won't experience some guilt, but there will at least be a way of arguing back against the guilt in their head, and not letting it dominate their life.

Of course, I have to point out that this is one way of looking at guilt at a level of coping and personal morality; different professional, legal or religious systems may view things differently.

Sometimes, the best thing we can do with our guilt – especially if it is deserved or rational guilt – is to acknowledge it, learn the lesson it teaches carefully (e.g. 'In future I won't take for granted the support of the people who care for me') and try to move on. Unending personal misery doesn't actually put right past wrongs, and though some level of punishment may be in order, guilt can soon become corrosive, and sometimes even self-indulgent.

A final way of dealing with guilt is to make amends in some way. This is a key part in some recovery programmes for people with addiction problems to drink or drugs. Step 9 of the Alcoholics Anonymous twelve-step plan is 'make direct amends to the people you have harmed except when to do so would injure them or others'.[79] If successful, the advantages are clear – facing the reality of our bad behaviour, some benefit to the wronged party, and a sense of actually earning forgiveness. There are risks, however: reopening old wounds can hurt the other party (hence the caution in Step 9, above), and there is no guarantee that they will anyway react the way you hoped. We need to ask ourselves who we're doing this for; if we create more pain for others in making ourselves feel better, then perhaps we give ourselves another good reason for feeling guilty!

## Shame

Shame is a close relative of guilt (we often use 'ashamed' more or less interchangeably with it).[80] Shame doesn't necessarily imply a moral judgement; we might feel shame for being the worst-performing member of a team, even when everyone recognises we have tried our hardest. Also, while guilt is something we can feel in private, shame generally requires there to be others around (or for us to be anticipating there being others around). This is because it is often tied up with belief (accurate or otherwise) that others will think poorly of us – for having been dumped, for having failed at business, for our appearance (e.g. people staring after a disfiguring injury).

Sometimes, of course, it may be that you've got it wrong, that no one is actually aware of, or cares about, the thing you're shamed by. Or it may be that you can manage to dismiss their opinion – so what if they think I'm a weakling/failure/freak; why should I give a damn about their opinion?

When you can't do that it may be best to acknowledge the presence of shame, and the reason for it, and take a hard look at what you do about living with it. Is it a question of just dealing with the reactions of others until they (let's hope) forget about it? Or do you want to avoid all circumstances where people might know about it – perhaps avoid going back to that particular nightclub, or move to a different town? That should really be a last resort, since (as tempting an impulse as it may be when the sense of shame is crushing) the costs of avoidance can be great, and it might not be how you want to live your life. On the other hand I've known people get to that stage and see it as a 'clean break', enabling them to get on with their life.

> If Peter was honest with himself, one of the best things about having his own business was how it made him feel about himself. He'd always liked the idea of being an entrepreneur, and found himself mixing with a lot of people who ran their own companies at the local Rotary Club. In fact, since setting his business up, he'd talked to them about little else, and enjoyed holding forth about the best business loans, discussing market trends and comparing accountants. When it was becoming clear that his business wasn't taking off in the way he'd have liked, he tried to talk a more confident outlook than he felt. When the collapse came, Peter simply couldn't face talking to those same people; he thought back to how positive – boastful even – he'd been with them, and felt they'd be laughing behind his back at his fall. A couple of times he was determined to go along to a club meeting but found an excuse at the last minute not to attend. Finally, he accepted that the stress of seeing them all was just too much in addition to everything else he was facing, and sent a brief letter stating that he was leaving the club due to pressure of outside commitments. He feels better for doing that, but still becomes anxious if he catches sight of one of his acquaintances around town.

But if you're not being that extreme, and accept that you will have to face others, it may be worthwhile following one of the ideas in Chapter 6, and prepare carefully exactly what you're going to say to others about the situation. Of course, you can't control what they'll say back, but at least you can take a little control over the situation, so that you're less likely to end up reduced to red-faced mumbling in front of others. And sometimes, a combination of the passage of time and a different outlook can enable you to look people in the eye again.

A couple of very difficult years later, Peter's bankruptcy has been settled, he's completed his prison sentence, and his family have moved into smaller rented accommodation. Times are much tougher, but he's doing his best to rebuild his life. To his horror, he finds himself standing next to one of his old Rotary Club acquaintances in a queue, and can't really avoid talking to him. There is some awkwardness to begin with, but the other businessman is soon asking genuinely interested questions about the process of Peter's financial collapse. At his invitation, Peter takes the decision not simply to go back to the club one more time, but actually give a presentation entitled 'Death of a small business: a cautionary tale'. Preparing and delivering it forces him to confront all those events, but from a distance; he isn't running away from their memories any more. The presentation is well received, giving one of the first boosts to his self-esteem in a long time. Peter doesn't go back to the club again, but feels that he doesn't need to, and he no longer fears anyone knowing about his story.

As well as the question of how best to behave towards others, there is also the question of how to behave towards yourself; for one of the hallmarks of shame is self-criticism, even sometimes self-loathing. It is developing the ability to feel kindness towards oneself even in the presence of difficulty that greater strength and resilience can emerge.

If you're recognising these feelings, you may want to investigate an approach called compassionate mind training. As the name implies, this method looks at developing the individual's ability to extend towards him- or herself some of the warmth, empathy and acceptance that they probably already show to (some) others, and in so doing replace the self-attacking tendencies with a more understanding and soothing approach.[81] In many ways, compassionate mind training is a 'fellow traveller' with mindfulness and acceptance-based treatments, and together they have been seen as a 'new wave' of cognitive and behavioural therapies, which we'll discuss in Chapter 9.

## Hope

Why would hope be on the list of emotions to be dealt with? The psychologically pedantic (and that would cover me and most of my profession!) might quibble with calling hope an emotion at all. In many ways it's more a class of belief, the belief that a desired outcome may come about. Yet hope can certainly give a person strength and energy, and keep their mood from dropping despite adversity, and when you talk to people about hope, they will often agree that there is a feeling associated with it.[82] At work, I get to talk about hope – and its fragility – quite a lot; the moment at which your consultant tells you that there's no longer a chance of cure or long-term control and that the focus now is on managing symptoms and quality of life, is often when palliative care services become involved. Patients and family members will sometimes talk about all hope having gone. Equally, others maintain unwavering hope of a good outcome (whatever that means for them) irrespective of what their doctors are telling them.

Or, you might feel that hope is such a positive thing that it requires nurturing at all costs, not 'managing'. Some people would argue that hope, even hope for something unlikely, can be the only thing that keeps a person going, and even that it can keep a person alive. Well, perhaps (though the evidence in cancer is broadly against that),[83] but hope has its darker side too.

On one of the rare occasions that he has opened up fully to someone else (his sister), Anil admits that the relationship with Sarah has been grinding him down for years. He feels she doesn't take him seriously, doesn't share his values or want the same things in life, and can be very belittling. The affair (or maybe affairs) show that she doesn't value him or his feelings. There's no trust, no fun, and nowhere to go in the relationship.

So why, asks his sister, has he put up with it so long?

Anil thinks about it, and replies that it's because he's always hoped that one day things will go back to being how they used to be; and while he hopes for that, he can't bring himself to let go.

Anil had, in effect, allowed himself to become a prisoner of hope.

Sometimes people see hope as powerful in itself – that hoping enough for something will make it come true; even that if they want it enough, they are somehow *entitled* to it coming true. See how often on TV talent shows rejected contestants can't see past their having wanted stardom since the age of five in order to realise that they genuinely are tone-deaf; it's as if that minor fact shouldn't matter so long as you really, really want it. And the crushing disappointment on their faces after rejection points out one of the costs of hope.

It's true that there is evidence that maintaining some degree of hope is vital for psychological well-being, and can even affect some aspects of a person's health; or rather, looking at the reverse, the loss of all hope does seem associated with depression, suicide risk and certain types of poorer health outcomes.[84]

So here's our paradox; we need hope, but unrealistic hope can have devastating results – yet as hope always refers to future events, we can never be certain of exactly how realistic our hopes are!

One way of approaching this is similar to an idea we looked at back in Chapter 2, that at any given point there is a range of possible future outcomes, some better than others, some likelier than others. As we can't know for sure which path the future will follow, maybe the best we can do is be aware of some of the key ones (e.g. best plausible outcome, worst plausible outcome, a couple of likely outcomes in between) – this establishes the likely range of possibilities.

> The week before his fraud trial, Peter had met with his barrister. After dealing with some details of how they would approach the case in court, Peter asked the question most on his mind – what was likely to happen to him? With a crispness based on long practice, his barrister answered, 'Can't say for certain; best case would be we get you off on a technicality, worst case probably three years mainstream prison; more likely would be around one year mostly lower-grade prison, back home within six months.' Though it was a shock to hear it said so baldly, at least Peter could start preparing his family for his being away for quite a while.

Peter could now choose to follow the old adage of 'hope for the best and prepare for the worst'. Just because he was acting on the probability of a prison sentence doesn't mean that he could not also allow himself to hope for an acquittal. Taking account of the range of possibilities maintains realism while allowing hope. It tends to be when people single-mindedly only allow themselves to look at the best possible outcome (as Anil did earlier in this section) that problems arise.

A final point to make here is that hope itself sometimes matters more than the specific thing being hoped for; even when we need to let go of a hope, there will always be something else we can hope for instead; the key to coping with apparent loss of hope is often to find a new and plausible target for it. In my palliative care work, people who have just discovered that their condition is now incurable and will certainly lead to death often (understandably) find that news devastating, and will talk about all hope having gone. This in turn can easily lead to a period of lower mood or even outright depression, and many will describe a feeling of hopelessness. Yet with the support of their family and friends, and sometimes professionals, they will often start hoping for, and working towards, a new target – living long enough to attend an upcoming family wedding, having good symptom control, or dying at home rather than in hospital. And even some of these will need to be abandoned, or amended; yet hope as an entity need never be lost permanently.[85]

And for some, of course, specific religious beliefs offer hope for things beyond death – of going to a better place, of reunion with loved ones who have already died. Where people genuinely and firmly hold such beliefs, they can undoubtedly be a comfort. However, for the many who are experiencing doubts at such a time, or never had such beliefs in the first place, having others suggest this kind of hope can be unwelcome and aggravating; so in supporting someone, it's always better to follow their lead on such matters rather than offering your own opinion.

At a broader level, those with strong religious beliefs may find their faith offers ways of dealing with strong emotions: perhaps reading the relevant holy texts, discussing the situation with a trusted faith leader or undertaking the rituals and practices of that religion. For some people, however, times of crisis actually make them feel less in touch with those particular beliefs, and therefore less able to benefit from the religious structures and practices around them. So it may well be too simplistic to say that religious faith is either a straightforwardly good or straightforwardly bad thing to have in a crisis.[86]

## Happiness

> Happiness is not a goal; it is a by-product.
>
> Eleanor Roosevelt

If it initially seemed odd that 'hope' needed to be handled carefully, then 'happiness' might seem even more certainly an unreservedly good thing. It seems to be a fairly universal goal, and its pursuit is famously enshrined in the US constitution. And I've certainly nothing against happiness – indeed I'm a big fan of it. But there are still one or two things to be said on the subject.

The problem isn't so much what happiness is like when it's present; it's more that it never seems to last. Even when life is going really well – you've got the things that are held to confer happiness (health, good relationships, security, pleasant activities, nice things) – it's rare to feel positively happy for days or weeks on end. And, given how entrenched the pursuit of happiness is, the automatic response is to try to get more happiness. Getting more health, or more security, or even better relationships, isn't always easily done, so we tend to focus on doing more of the pleasant activities (e.g. going on holidays) or getting more nice things (gadgets, handbags, new toys). Unfortunately, they cost money, so we either feel frustrated that we can't get them (making us feel less happy) or we work harder and longer hours to earn the money, giving ourselves less time to enjoy our nice things, and creating more stress and tiredness, making us unhappy. So constantly seeking happiness can lead us into traps.[87]

But what if that whole cycle is based on a misunderstanding of what happiness actually *is*?

I tend to contrast happiness with contentment. Happiness is more intense, euphoric and often short-lived. Contentment is calmer, less obvious, but seems as if it can be a more stable state (allowing for the fact that any emotional state will sooner or later be interrupted by another one). The analogy I often make is with acceleration and speed. If you're in a car or an aircraft, you can really notice acceleration – you're aware of it pinning you back in your seat as you change from travelling at 30 mph to travelling at 70 as you join a motorway; it's even more vivid when you go from stationary to 175 mph in a jumbo as it heads for take-off. Yet when you reach a steady speed, you can't feel it; the jet cruising at 550 mph feels as if it's not moving. So acceleration is much more noticeable than speed. My analogy is that happiness is like acceleration, contentment is like speed; we feel happiness intensely when we're moving from things being bad to things being good. But when those good things are established and we're getting on with living with them, then that's like reaching a steady cruising speed – we don't *feel* it any more, and we don't notice it, despite the fact that reaching that speed was the whole point of doing the accelerating. If we take the time to notice what we're now doing, then we can be content, but we can't rely on being passively taken over by happiness, because we're not accelerating any more. And here's the rub: if we wrongly think that happiness is something we can feel the whole time or – even worse – that feeling constantly happy should be the norm, then we're going to seek that feeling by trying to accelerate more and more – something that is obviously not sustainable, and can be self-destructive. It's not hard to see how that relates to seeking more and more wealth, fame, or drug-induced highs.

And the relevance of this way of looking at happiness and contentment? In dealing with personal disasters, there may sometimes be happy moments amid the stressful and the sad; when something goes right for once, or we take pleasure from something unconnected with the crisis. That kind of happiness will make itself known clearly enough, and we should relish every moment of it. But, crucially, we shouldn't be expecting to feel like that all the time, and shouldn't become addicted to doing things just because they fleetingly bring it on. What we can look to experience longer is contentment, but *look* is the operative term – it requires noticing those things that are good, pleasant or just OK in our lives, and recognising their value to us – how much worse things would be without them. If that sounds too much like 'counting your blessings', then I apologise, but there genuinely is some wisdom in that old principle. In the disastrous situations we are talking about, there is plenty of bad stuff happening, but recognising and valuing any positives becomes all the more vital if we are to bear the apparently unbearable, and try to get on with life as best we can despite the bad stuff.

## Key points

- Emotional responses are natural in extreme situations. We might not be able to stop them, but there are things we can do to stop them taking over, or to stop our minds from making them even worse.
- Emotions may well be deserved, and we should give a little respect to someone's right to feel sad, or scared, or angry when things are going badly.

- Excessive sadness can be dealt with by distraction, activity, positive events, exercise, or carefully challenging negative thoughts.
- Anxiety or fear-based emotions (including worry) are wired into us as responses to threat, via the fight–flight instinct. Yet excessive worry makes it harder to cope as it rarely solves problems.
- To stop ourselves being overwhelmed by worry, we need to give some controlled time for worrying, but otherwise recognise the difference between worry (temporary mental event) and the thing the worry is about.
- Relaxation, absorbing activity, complementary therapies, yoga and its relatives, visualisation, hypnosis and meditation provide useful tools for tackling anxiety.
- Anger can be like a volcano – building up pressure (often from different sources) then exploding suddenly. Yet there are generally warning signs.
- Learn to spot the situations that routinely wind you up, work out what you're *actually* angry about and learn ways of calming down (relaxing, counting in your head, burning it off).
- Guilt can be corrosive; is it deserved? Are you actually responsible for the event? Learn the lessons and move on. Beware of making yourself feel better but causing others more pain in the process.
- Shame: after time has passed, do you want to face up to others, or avoid them? Take an active decision about it.
- Hope can be positive, but don't be a prisoner of hope. If you're hoping for something that's not going to happen, find something more realistic to hope for (and work towards) instead – otherwise you're dooming yourself to failure and disappointment.
- We all tend to seek happiness, but maybe it's not an emotion we can feel all the time; contentment may be a more sustainable feeling to aspire to (remember the analogy of acceleration and speed).
- For those with strong religious beliefs, reflection on the relevant texts, discussion with a faith leader or performing religious practices can often (though not always) help.

# 9

# The eye of the storm

## Finding a quieter place in the middle of it all

To return to our image of a life crisis being like a storm; we've seen that there's no way of preventing or stopping that storm ourselves, and in Chapter 8 the emphasis has been upon riding it as best we can. One of the difficulties here is that the constant buffeting can be hard to endure, and blow us a long way off course. Would it be possible to find some equivalent of the eye of a hurricane, where the storm is still going on around us, but (for a time at least) we can be in a calmer place, and take stock of which way we want to be heading even if the winds do pick up again?

Perhaps this 'quieter place in the middle of it all' isn't so much a location we have to find, but rather is a consequence of taking a different approach at times.

Many of the ways of coping that we've discussed so far have been aimed at the kind of effect most of us would be looking for – sorting out confusion, reducing troubling thoughts, calming unpleasant emotions and so on. It's what we could call a 'control agenda', and it seems fairly automatic to most of us to react to problems that way (or, at least, wish we could react that way). And when it works, it works.

But, as I've mentioned previously, there are a couple of problems that can crop up with these ways of responding: sometimes they don't work, and often they make some aspects of the situation worse.

Throughout Helen's illness, her partner Keith has managed to keep himself going by focusing on positive and optimistic thoughts. Whenever thoughts about her doing less well (or even dying) have intruded, he's searched through his memory for any encouraging words the doctors have used, or news stories he's read about people who had unexpectedly recovered from a poor prognosis. And if that hasn't worked, he's forced himself to plan his next day at work in fine detail to prevent his mind dwelling on sad or terrifying thoughts. But as Helen has got more ill, it's become harder and harder to dismiss or escape those awful thoughts, and the attempt to do so grows more exhausting. His sleep – already disturbed by attending to Helen's symptoms and medication – is further interrupted by the mental battle to think positively. When Helen's community nurse notices how tired he looks, he ends up confessing what his night-times have turned into; she tells him what he has already begun to guess, that he has to find a different way of dealing with this.

The last couple of decades have seen researchers and therapists addressing this problem, coming from widely different areas (e.g. treating people with frequent relapses into depression, or chronic physical pain, or people with personality disorders) and from different therapeutic backgrounds. Yet they more-or-less independently seem to keep hitting on the same idea, that sometimes the important thing isn't changing the problem, it's learning to 'accept' events, thoughts and feelings as they are, and not struggling so much against them. And instead of either getting caught up in those thoughts and feelings or trying to control them, learn instead to simply pay attention to what's happening to us in the present moment – a skill known as mindfulness.

These themes of acceptance and mindfulness are a common factor in what have been called the 'third wave' of cognitive and behavioural therapies, and I think they have a lot of benefits in the situations we've been discussing. So, I plan to introduce two of those approaches: first mindfulness, then acceptance and commitment therapy.

## Being in the present: mindfulness

In Chapter 8, we looked in some detail at difficult and often unpleasant emotional states, and elsewhere we've considered intrusive thoughts and unwanted physical sensations. The problem is that any of these can capture our attention, dominate it, and before we know it we've not thought of anything else for minutes or even hours.

Wouldn't it be better if we were able to spot quickly when our mind was going off onto something unhelpful, and rather than focusing on that, stay on whatever we wanted to be thinking about or experiencing? That's a key part of using mindfulness as an approach to dealing with life. It has its roots in eastern thinking, but is increasingly applied within western healthcare systems, where there is good evidence of its ability to help people deal with a wide range of chronic health problems,[88] including long-term pain,[89] multiple sclerosis,[90] recurrent major depression,[91] and (the original reason for my interest) cancer.[92]

It uses a series of mental exercises (some people prefer to use the original term 'meditation') to develop people's abilities to focus their attention on a place of their choosing, and notice when the mind is drawn away by sounds, sensations, thoughts or feelings. The important thing then is not to regard such mind-wandering as failure, and not to get involved in whatever the mind has wandered to, but simply to recognise and accept its presence, and then gently but firmly bring the attention back to the chosen focus (often the sensations of breathing, but it can be many other things too). Superficially, that might sound like an effective form of thought-blocking, but in reality there is a large component of accepting that unwelcome things are present, and simply continuing despite them.

If some of this sounds familiar, it might be because elements of it have already shown up several times in this book, especially in Chapter 8, when we were talking about anxiety and worry. Back there, we looked at the destructive effect of prolonged worrying, and how keeping the mind 'in the present' can alleviate the suffering this causes.

Again, though, I should emphasise that mindfulness is not simply a way of avoiding things; we talk about it having two main components of *awareness* and *acceptance*. Learning to control awareness is a useful coping tool, but it is only with the increased ability to accept our feelings, thoughts, bodily sensations and situation in general that the fuller benefits become apparent.

There is a children's game ('Othello') that was marketed with the slogan 'a minute to learn, a lifetime to master'. Well, mindfulness certainly takes longer than a minute to learn – an eight-week course with daily home practice is the standard introduction. And though you might apply it for a lifetime, I doubt the keenest practitioner would claim to have completely 'mastered' the ability to accept that which is present and stay in touch with everything that is happening in this present moment. But then it does represent a fundamental shift in our attitudes to the world – away from frantically trying to do everything, make everything right, cling on to what is good and push away what is bad. And living in the real world as we do, that's going to be a constant balancing act.

Yet for many of those who decide to adopt this approach (and it certainly doesn't suit everyone), the gains in calmness, mood, quality of life and well-being (including management of symptoms like insomnia and fatigue)[93] may be worth the investment of effort. However, starting it in the middle of a major crisis is not ideal; mindfulness is a practice for every day, and its benefits in crisis will be better if the practice is already established. As Jon Kabat-Zinn (one of the founders of this approach) says, you need to weave your parachute every day, not just when the plane is about to crash!

You can get a taste of this approach by trying out the following exercise – a variation of classic mindfulness practices which I use a lot with clients. Read it through carefully a couple of times before trying it, so you can remember what to do at each stage (it doesn't work so well if you're keeping one eye open to read the next part of the instruction).

### *Here and now exercise*

- Sit somewhere you can be undisturbed for the next ten minutes or so. Settle into a comfortable but reasonably upright position (slouching could become uncomfortable).
- Let your gaze wander the room until you find something to look at – it doesn't really matter what, could be a chair, light fitting, patch of carpet, or anything. Now really look at it, notice its colour, variation of light and shade, texture, lines and angles. After 30 seconds or so, say inside your head, 'Right here and now, I'm seeing a [*whatever you're looking at*].'
- Then move your gaze onto something else and repeat the process, ending with 'Right here and now, I'm seeing a . . .' And then do it a third time.
- Next allow your eyes to close, and pay attention to what you can hear. Select one sound, and notice in detail its qualities – how loud or soft, whether it's constant or changing, whether your mind judges it pleasant or unpleasant. Then say in your head, 'Right here and now, I'm hearing [*whatever the sound is*].' Then find another sound, and do the same. And then a third; that might be tricky, but listen carefully and there's often more than you've noticed.
- Now switch your attention to the sense of touch. Find something that you can feel in contact with you – could be clothing against skin, the chair underneath you, socks against feet or anything else. Really notice what it feels like, then say to yourself, 'Right here and now, I'm feeling [*whatever the sensation is*].' Let go of that sensation of touch, and find another; same drill. Then a third.
- This time, find a sensation anywhere within your body. It doesn't have to be significant, it could just be any feelings you can detect inside your foot, calf, stomach, or shoulders, and it doesn't matter

whether it's pleasant, unpleasant or neutral, we're just interested in giving you practice in noticing. Then say, 'Right here and now, I'm feeling [*whatever the sensation is*].' Then move onto a second, then a third. Don't give up if you think you can't find anything to feel inside; at worst move an arm or leg and notice what that feels like.

- Now turn your attention to your breath; just notice whatever there is to notice about the sensation of breathing. Don't try to change anything about your breathing, just let it carry on at whatever pace and depth it wants to. You might be most aware of it in your mouth and nose as breath enters and leaves your body, or in your chest as the lungs fill and empty, or in your stomach as it moves to make room for the lungs filling and emptying. For a couple of minutes, just rest your attention on your breath. And when your mind wanders – which it surely will – simply notice where it's gone to, and gently bring it back to this breath, here and now.
- After a couple of minutes of this, take two intentionally deeper breaths, and allow your eyes to open again.
- So to recap, it's three things I see, three things I hear, three things I feel (from the outside), three things I feel (from the inside), then focus on the breath.

There are several things you may have noticed while doing that. You may not feel any calmer or more relaxed. Well, that's not the aim. Nice if you do, but really not the aim; it's actually just noticing what's going on that matters. If we strive for any particular feeling, we actually add pressure.

You may have noticed just how much is going on around you and inside that you don't normally notice. That sensation in your stomach, the ticking of the clock – they were both always there, but your mind had been too tied up with other things to notice. So much of the detail in life is simply passing by without you noticing; and, sure, it might be overwhelming to be 'tuned in' to everything, all of the time, but it can be good to sample what's going on at times. For instance, if you were enjoying walking on a beach, you could get even more out of the experience by really noticing the sand under your toes, the breeze against your skin, the sound of waves on pebbles. It can also be useful as a 'grounding' technique when you are feeling totally swamped by thoughts and feelings (though it shouldn't be constantly used as a way of avoiding all unwanted experiences).

You may also have noticed how much your mind wanders, or chatters at you. Here's the paradox – that's not failure, that's simply how minds are. Although you were setting out to focus your attention on one thing at a time, the real gain here is the practice in spotting when your mind has drifted off. So, perversely, each time you go through the cycle of 'mind wanders – spot mind has wandered – notice where it's gone to – bring it back' is another strengthening of your mindfulness skills!

So why should this present-moment focusing on the breath, sounds, or whatever help a person cope in the face of a significant crisis? It goes back to something we discussed earlier (in Chapter 8), that the amount of time we are actually having to do things about a crisis is generally lower than the amount of time we are having thoughts about it. Moreover, those thoughts are often about things that have already happened, or might happen in the future; a recent study found that around half the time, our minds are on the past or future (rather than the present moment), and further that a wandering mind tends to cause its owner to become more unhappy.[94] So time spent attending to the present moment, and recognising whether the mind is wandering away, seems to pay off.

For anyone interested in pursuing this, there are suggested books in the Further Reading section at the end of the book, some of which include CDs of different mindfulness exercises.

A misunderstanding sometimes arises about these mindfulness and acceptance-based approaches, that they suggest becoming entirely passive and simply putting up with whatever happens rather than taking positive action to change those things that can be changed. In fact, mindfulness approaches aim to give a clarity of mental state that should make it easier, not harder, to take the right next action. It's true, though, that mindfulness approaches by themselves tend not to tell you what the appropriate next action should be; and that's where another of the 'third wave' techniques comes in.

## Adding value(s): acceptance and commitment therapy

Although this approach has rather different roots from mindfulness, acceptance and commitment therapy (ACT – pronounced as a single word) shares an emphasis on 'present moment awareness'. It puts even greater emphasis on accepting rather than trying to change unwanted emotions, and on stepping back or 'defusing' from intrusive thoughts (we've already applied that ACT technique in Chapter 2).

Where it adds something rather different to other mindfulness approaches is in regard to Values (and I'll write the word with a capital V to clarify when I'm using it in this particular way). Within the ACT model, Values are the ways you want to be and to act in the world, the approaches to living that matter most to you. The therapist and writer Russ Harris describes them as 'what we want to stand for in life, how we want to behave, what sort of person we want to be, what sort of strengths and qualities we want to develop'.[95] So examples might be 'being loving', 'taking care of my body', 'being honest in dealing with others', 'being caring towards the people I love', 'being utterly ruthless in business dealings with others'. That last example isn't one I'd personally choose to live by, but it is as much an example of a Value as the first; it's not the role of ACT to judge whether a Value is good or bad, or to supply a set of 'approved' Values to live by. Rather, it aims to help a person identify what matters to them (their Values), to find how far they are managing to live by their Values, and help them start taking committed action towards living more fully according to those Values they have lost contact with.

The reason why I think this can be particularly helpful for someone going through a crisis is that it can take so much effort getting through each day that you can lose sense of purpose or direction, and then your Values can act as a compass, helping you choose where to put your effort. And if that sounds at all familiar, it might be because we looked at a similar idea in Chapter 5, with the analogy of walking across a cow field. It's not enough to focus on what is immediately around your feet; you also need to check occasionally that you are heading towards the gate or else you'll simply wander aimlessly. Now we can say that the direction you're choosing to head is shaped by your Values. And while you may spend most of the time dealing with what's happening here and now, you need to look up every now and again to check that all this here-and-now activity is actually taking you in the direction you want.

A few months on from the separation, Anil realises that his life isn't now so totally dominated by losing Sarah. He certainly isn't lying around his flat any more – in fact he's barely there as he's flung himself more and more into his work. The more senior role he accepted has meant longer hours anyway, but he also chooses to spend extra time preparing for meetings and putting reports together. It gives him a greater sense of achievement, brings praise from colleagues, and has got him an invitation to an overseas sales conference. Though not much extra cash, as his sister points out. That makes Anil wonder – why *is* he doing this? Eventually, he realises that it's partly the sense of team work and competition that he also enjoys on the five-a-side pitch, coupled with a respect for hanging onto a steady job in difficult times. But that makes him think about some of the things that he values but isn't doing anything towards at the moment, like being involved in family life, and learning new things. He vows to keep working hard, but also be sure to make time to visit his parents more often, and maybe finally take those guitar lessons he's always considered.

Anil's important realisation was that the increased work wasn't simply a useful distraction from the pain of losing his girlfriend, but was also serving Values that he found important. Yet it wasn't enough, as other Values were being neglected in the process, and they too needed some attention for him to have a broader sense of living a life of greater fulfilment and vitality.

---

### *Find a Value and ACT on it*

- First, consider important areas of life; these might include work (in its broadest sense, including home building or education), friends, social life, family and intimate relationships, leisure, personal philosophy (religious, spiritual, political) or any other areas that matter to you.
- Then, initially for just one of these, ask yourself: How do I want to conduct myself in this area? What qualities would I like others to realise I have in this aspect of my life?
- Note that a Value can't be a goal that you can achieve (e.g. 'Get married to a good person'), it has to be an ongoing quality of your behaviour (e.g. 'Be a loving and supportive partner'). And it does have to be about *your* behaviour, not how you'd like someone else or the world to be, because ultimately only your own behaviour is under your control.
- Now write that Value down on a sheet of paper (or your diary, mobile phone, email to yourself or whatever medium you prefer). Ask yourself, 'If I stuck by this Value from now on, would that seem like how I'd want to live my life?' If the answer's 'No', then you've not hit something that is truly your Value; it may be that you've written down something you think you 'ought' to value, or that others would approve of, rather than something that you want your life to be about. If so, try again until you find something that you would truly want to live by, even if no one else ever knew about it.

- Then set yourself some goals that you're willing to commit to pursuing. They should be realistic, they should be clearly 'in the service' of that Value (while not conflicting directly with other Values you hold, e.g. becoming a better provider for your family by robbing old ladies), and you should be serious about them. Write one goal that you'll aim to achieve within the year, one that you'll achieve within the month, and one (however small) that you'll do within the next 24 hours. And then do it (don't 'try' to do it, there is no 'try' – just do it).

- Lastly on that sheet/page/screen, consider what you're willing to experience if that's what it takes to live by this Value. Nothing comes for free, and taking committed action towards an important end will inevitably bring some unwanted thoughts (e.g. 'I can't do this', 'I'm making an idiot of myself', 'They'll hate me for being like this'), emotions (e.g. anxiety, embarrassment) and physical sensations (e.g. tiredness, butterflies in the stomach).

- And write that commitment down like this:
  'I will [name of goal], in the service of [name of Value], and will accept [name of unwanted thoughts/emotions/sensations] if that's what it takes.'
  So, an example might be:
  'I will visit the gym twice weekly in the service of looking after my health and staying fit and well enough to care for my family, and will accept tiredness, boredom on the treadmill and the thought that there are more entertaining things I could be doing if that's what it takes.'

- Keep your record of this, and go back to see whether you're achieving those goals, and also whether other choices you are making are compatible with that Value.

- Once you've got that running, try the same for another of the areas of your life that you considered at the beginning of this exercise.

> • Remember, though, that this is not about being virtuous, or gaining the approval of others; it is about *you* living the kind of life *you* want to.

It would be foolish to claim that making that kind of change is easy but it certainly is possible, and the principles and the activity we've just gone through can make a difference all by themselves. The trickiest part is often avoiding getting tangled up in unwanted thoughts and accepting unwanted feelings. Any of the mindfulness techniques we have looked at can help with that, but if you wanted to go into it in more depth then the ideal would be to see a therapist who uses this ACT approach. Guidance for finding someone is included in the Further Reading section at the end of the book, as are the titles of some good self-help books specifically targeted at this technique if the individual therapy route isn't appropriate.

To end this section on a personal note, since I first began hearing about the effects of mindfulness and acceptance for people with serious illnesses, I've spent more time investigating it, being trained in it, and indeed practising it. For someone with a fairly strict scientific background, the idea of using a form of meditation in my practice would at one time have seemed unthinkable. Yet it's become woven into much of my work (for instance, it combines particularly well with some aspects of cognitive therapy) – for three main reasons:

- The evidence from carefully conducted research is strong, and getting stronger.[96]
- I've seen the profound impact it's had on some of the people I've taught it to, and on myself.
- It fits with a reality of life that's true for all of us, but comes into sharpest function for people experiencing major crises: we can't stop all the bad stuff happening, or make the feelings go away – all we can do is to cope with it the best we can, and not let it take over our minds and our lives completely.

## Key points

- Attempts to defeat unwanted thoughts and emotions will often fail and can make the situation worse.
- More and more people are using techniques based on present-moment awareness ('mindfulness') and acceptance to deal with the pressures of life.
- Developing mindfulness skills generally requires practice of meditation-based techniques of noticing what is happening in the present moment, and recognising then stepping back from thoughts, sensations or emotions that pull the mind away.
- Acceptance and commitment therapy teaches additional techniques for this 'stepping back', and adds emphasis upon identifying and acting upon central Values.
- Values (if accurately identified) can act as a compass direction, helping us make choices about what to do that suit our purposes, rather than simply allowing ourselves to be buffeted by the pressures of dealing with the immediate crisis.

# 10

# Rebuilding from driftwood

## After the event (assuming you're there)

As we saw in Chapter 7, it can be hard to see beyond the disaster itself, yet there will be an aftermath. Even if the person at the centre of things is no longer around (died, emigrated, imprisoned), the people left behind will have to face the prospect of carrying on with life, despite the impact of the events they've just experienced.

This is true in palliative care; much of the activity of course ceases with the death of the patient, but not all, because there will usually be grieving family and/or friends left behind. So, dependent upon individual need, there is often some sort of bereavement care service to help people cope with grief and, when the time is right, start moving on with life.

### The nature of grief

We have a tendency to think of grief as effectively the same thing as bereavement – the words get used interchangeably. The distinction is important, though. *Bereavement* means the fact that someone important to you has died; *grief* refers to the range of reactions to a major loss in your life. So while bereavement is mainly used to talk about a death, grief can be for other losses – like a relationship, some aspect of health, your independence. In fact, it covers the whole process of getting used to any major and probably permanent change for the worse in your life. Of course, changes for the better can take some getting used to as well, but that's a different story.

So, given that the theme of this book is dealing with major changes for the worse in life, it will be worthwhile looking at what we've learned from dealing with grief in palliative care, and seeing how it fits with other types of loss.

> In the first weeks after Sarah finally left, Anil has felt that he's going mad. Most of the time – and especially at work – he's getting on fairly well, but then he's suddenly overwhelmed by sadness, or anger, and sometimes a kind of panic. These feelings can hang around for hours or pass within minutes. He finds himself seeking out reminders of Sarah (photographs, trivial items of hers left at the flat) and dwells on them for an entire evening, yet the next day tries to shut her out of his mind, or turn over the TV if there's someone looking at all like her. Friends invite him out and try to cheer him up, but even if he goes along, he often feels empty. Worst of all, having always been proud of how calm and reasonable he is, now Anil finds himself having moments of rage, even smashing items in his flat. And some of these experiences seem to be getting worse rather than better.

It's worth thinking first about the emotional impact of the loss. In Anil's case, the thing that worried him most was the range of different powerful emotions that could come and go at such short notice. As we discussed in Chapter 4, people sometimes talk about phases or stages of grief, which can imply that there should be an orderly sequence of experience, such as first denial, then anger, then despair, then acceptance. The problem with that sort of view (and one which the original authors of those models warned about) is that people's experiences often aren't like that. Sure, all of those states can happen, and for *some* people they happen in that sequence. Far more people, however, are like Anil and swing between different emotional states and periods of calm, and are as likely to jump back to earlier emotions as move smoothly on to the next predicted stage.

Perhaps the best advice that can be given is to accept that this period of intense and unpredictable emotions is going to be with you for a little while, and that will have implications for how emotionally robust you are, how ready for new challenges and new relationships. Sometimes (as the traditional grief theories predict) there can be an initial period which gets termed numbness, or denial, but is more like the calm before the storm. And yet, people being as individual as they are, for some that storm simply never comes even when the loss is huge; it's important to realise that possibility, because I've certainly met people who are terrified that there is something awfully wrong because they haven't started to grieve 'properly' yet. And some will indeed start to experience those intense emotions later than others, but others will simply move smoothly on with life with just the more manageable normal emotions of sadness, concern or frustration.

How long will it go on for? That's an unanswerable question. To some extent, grief for a very major loss can be lifelong, as the change is permanent, and there may be some element of a reaction to it for the rest of your life.[97] That doesn't mean you should expect always to feel the way you do in the first couple of weeks or months after a loss, but rather that at some points (anniversaries, family events, being confronted with reminders) there may be a brief period of strong emotion again. By and large, the profile is that as time passes periods of very strong emotion get shorter and less frequent; they also usually get less intense, but at their peak they can still be very strong.

Grief also affects how we see the past; if it's been a death, then that may be how we remember life with the person who's died. But it needn't just be death.

In the months since Debbie's factory closed, she's found it hard to take it all in. That job was central to her life for so long, and there were those few months of headlines, uncertainties, visits by concerned-looking local MPs; the day after she brought home her family photos and personal tools it seemed unreal. She feels oddly calm about it all, to the extent that friends assume she's coping really well, and fellow church members attribute it to her faith. Yet Debbie finds herself unable to look at the factory, read the feature in the local paper about its long history, and certainly can't swap stories with the other newly unemployed colleagues about the good old days. For though she was very happy there, and it felt like another home to her, all she can think of now are the union meetings about the closure, the hours of uncertainty about the future, and the memory of the first time she saw the news item about possible closure. It's as if memories of all those good years there have become contaminated by the misery of the last couple of months.

Compared to the practical and financial problems someone in Debbie's situation is facing, being unable to think about happy memories may seem insignificant, but it can be difficult if the thing lost was an important relationship, a source of self-esteem or (as in Debbie's case) a substantial part of your life and social contact. These connections with life before the loss (be they memories, or actually dealing with things from your previous life) do matter, because they were important parts of your life. It is always a risky business making predictions about how things will go for people in the future, but it is frequently the case that in the immediate aftermath of a loss, the enormity of the events towards the end overwhelms other memories or associations with the thing that has been lost. As time begins to pass, people are often able to remember happier times, but that thought then automatically links to memories of how it ended and the sadness of loss. Eventually, though, most people get to the stage that, while they will never forget the circumstances of their loss, they are able to think about happier (or more neutral) memories, without necessarily going on to anything sadder. But there's probably not much a person can do to speed that process along.

Another way in which thinking about grief has changed over the years is about 'letting go' of the past. Who can forget the moving scene in that subtle exploration of attachment and grief, *Top Gun*, where Maverick finally symbolically 'lets go' of his deceased co-pilot by throwing his dog-tags into the sea, so allowing himself to get on with his life of flying jets and playing volleyball. I think the idea of a single moment of 'letting go' being followed by moving on with life is flawed in several ways. First, most changes in grief are lengthy, stop–start affairs with leaps forwards and setbacks. Second, we're moving on with life from the start of grief – because we swing like a pendulum between moments of being consumed by the loss and periods of facing the future – sorting out finances, making new arrangements, learning new skills and so on.[98] And third, because we probably don't actually 'let go' of someone (or, I'd argue, something) we've really loved; they carry on being a part of our lives even if only in our heads (and, metaphorically, our hearts).

Traditional talk of getting over the grief and leaving the deceased person behind just doesn't seem to fit most people's experience. It seems to be more a case of them having a different role in our lives; we think about them occasionally or often, remember them at times with sadness and at times happily, we talk to them once in a while (out loud or in our heads) and we can even work out what they'd have thought about us moving house, changing job, or even starting a new relationship. These get called 'continuing bonds',[99] and I'd argue that they don't just apply to bereavement, but fit with other major changes in life.

Debbie eventually gets a job at the local supermarket, much less well paid than she was at the factory, but a job nonetheless. Her inability to talk about life at the factory continues for a while – when she meets ex-colleagues she focuses instead on what they're up to now. As time passes, though, she occasionally finds herself talking about things that happened there. When some of the other former employees form a community action group to lobby for facilities for the local youth to be part of the redevelopment of the old factory site, she's keen to join. Two years later, she runs a newsletter for women who used to work there, and bores her daughter endlessly with the lessons of hard graft, teamwork and camaraderie that she learnt at the factory. That's only a small part of her life alongside learning to be a supervisor at the supermarket, and her church work. But it's a part of her life that she can now look back on fondly, with only occasional bouts of regret and anger. And those feelings she can deal with.

There's a practical implication – actually a potential benefit – from these continuing bonds. Some will even be able to work out what that person would have thought and said about a particular decision or dilemma ('Should I move house?' 'Should I get a new job?'); it's not emotionally the same as having that person there, but if you're missing their advice and opinion, remember you could probably second-guess them when they were alive, so (once the immediate, raw months have passed) why not do so now?

My personal opinion is that, much of the time, our relationship with a living person is actually a relationship with our own mental representation of them, rather than the person themselves. Imagine a situation where you're watching TV with your partner, or a close friend. If they leave the room to make a cup of tea, you still know how they would probably react if something they particularly like or hate comes on. That's because you carry an internal model (or simulation) of them in your mind. This is another example of the kind of mental representations we discussed in Chapter 3. While mental representations can get obscured by the pain of grief, they actually don't go away just because someone has died, so neither need the relationship, so long as it can change to take account of the reality of that person no longer being present.

We've been talking a lot about the pain of loss, and relating that mainly to the loss of a person in bereavement; that's where most of the models, the research and the experience come from. But it also comes in useful in considering how, for example, people respond to losing their family in a separation, or losing their sight. Again, it may not be possible to suppress the memory that you were ever sighted, or someone with a family; instead it may be a balance between accepting the reality of the loss, remembering that the previous existence was a big part of your life and beginning to build a new life around the circumstances and limitations you find yourself with now.

Of course, building that new life is a massively complex undertaking itself, and it requires many things.

### Understanding of the situation that you now find yourself in

Changes have consequences that may not be apparent. That criminal conviction for fraud may have a cascade of effects on your ability to get another job, apply for finance and so on, and these may then impact on your financial ability to live how you used to. Suddenly, getting through the week with a roof still over your head and food on the table may require planning and effort in a way it never did before, and shopping to a tight budget at markets or discount super-markets is a different experience from simply choosing whatever takes your fancy at a department store.

We considered this in Chapter 4. The key point to reinforce is that what will work *now* is likely to be very different from what worked in life prior to the disaster. We talked then about 'playing the hand you've got'. There's another analogy I use, particularly for families who are losing or have lost a parent, and it relates to chairs. Chairs usually have four legs, and they're set out in a pattern that gives the best stability (generally speaking one in each corner of the seat area). Take one of those legs away, and the chair becomes unstable. Yet a three-legged chair can be almost as stable as a four-legged one (think of a milking stool), *provided* that the positions of the three chair legs are changed in relation to each other. That's a very basic – simplistic perhaps – analogy, and there's a whole field of family therapy[100] (or, more generally, 'systemic therapy') that deals with the subtle complexities of how relationships between members of a group adapt – or fail to – after a change such as losing a group member. But the principle remains the same, that when a parent dies, a spouse gets sent to prison, an inspirational business leader gets poached by another company, or the lead singer of a band decides to go solo, the relationships between everyone left behind will probably have to change at least to some extent, to function well in the absence of that person. In part, that's because the chance of someone or something slotting in exactly the same niche, and behaving in exactly the same manner, as the previous occupant is almost zero.

### Getting used to it

We've looked at this in some detail in Chapters 3 and 4, including the fact that it takes a while for the new reality to sink in. However, then we were getting used to the idea of something bad being about to happen – now we're living with the reality of it. And strangely enough, many people find that almost a relief. Living under the shadow of impending disaster becomes exhausting, and once events have happened and we're dealing with the consequences (however drastic they are) there is at least sometimes a sense that you can at last get on and do something. I've certainly come across many patients who have been waiting for a firm diagnosis for a long time; when it comes, even though it is very bad, they report a sense of relief that the uncertainty and waiting are over, and they at last know what they're up against.

### Facing major decisions

As we've seen throughout the book, even though some things get thrust on you, there are often big decisions to be faced. That was discussed in detail back in Chapter 5, but there's one thing to add regarding decisions to be made in the aftermath. It's almost a cliché that the newly bereaved are advised 'don't make any big decisions at the moment'. And of course, that's sound advice in principle; immediately after a death it may be so painful to face any reminders of the person you've lost that there's a temptation to hide from their things, move house, move town. Yet, a few months later, the bereaved person might regret such actions, as they are becoming more ready to deal with their grief, and may want to be in contact with those very things that they've run away from.

The big problem is that some major decisions can't wait – choices may have to be made very soon after a loss or disaster. New housing may have to be found, decisions made about winding up a business, or about relationships with others. And they're having to be faced while you are still trying to adjust to all the changes and their effects inside you – there may be uncertainty, loss of confidence, difficulty concentrating, mood swings. And the problems may be worsened by the very absence of the person who's died; you don't have their advice, and perhaps they usually made such decisions. Remember what we discussed above, though: sometimes, you may be able to work out what that person would have thought had they been here. You don't have to agree with them, of course, but at least you might not feel so much that the decision is all down to you.

In terms of advice, perhaps all that we can do is try to work out which big decisions can safely be deferred, and for those that cannot, seek and listen to the advice of those we trust most, remembering that the ultimate decision is our own. And, crucially, if that decision doesn't turn out for the best, we mustn't beat ourselves up about it, because that was the best decision we could make in the situation we actually found ourselves in.

## The support of others

We've just touched on one way in which we might look for the support of others (advice), and there may be other types of support we can seek. But even if we are lucky enough to have others around, there are limitations we have to be aware of, because at some point we are going to feel let down by someone – and possibly many people. It may be that there's nothing we can do to prevent that, but if we're at least aware of some of the reasons behind it, then at least we'll be less prone to jump to the conclusion that the other person is being malicious or purposely hurtful.

### *Limits of their understanding*

If someone else is not in your shoes, then they aren't going to know the full impact of the situation. They may be able to see the obvious effects, but not be in a position to grasp how far the ripples spread out. The consequence can be that genuinely meant attempts to help are not only useless, but actually make you feel worse.

> After Helen's death, her partner Keith struggles. Within a few weeks he is back at work, and young Liam is generally fed, dressed and at school when he is meant to be. But those moments (especially late at night) when Keith isn't busy are full of loneliness and pain, and even at work the odd red-eyed moment makes it clear to his friends that times are still tough. To help cheer him up, they invite him on a weekend away to see a football match, spend the evening drinking and go paintballing the next day. What they haven't even thought about is how he'd manage the childcare – which drives home to him yet again how everything rests on his shoulders, and how some things he used to enjoy just can't be part of his life right now.

### *Their expectations and judgements*

How a person looks at a situation depends as much upon the person as the situation. This means that another person may have a very different approach to dealing with a crisis. So the people around you when you are in crisis are bound to have different ideas of what should be done. Now, there's often a difference between how people *think* they would deal with a situation compared to how they actually deal with it when the time comes. And it's certainly tempting, when offered unhelpful advice, to think, 'What do they know about it?' But by remembering that the other person may genuinely have a different approach, which (maybe) would work for them even if not for you, you might avoid getting too wound up. Sometimes, the best support comes from those who are most sparing with advice.

## Limits of patience

Dealing with a person in crisis, perhaps in distress and possibly needing practical as well as emotional support can take up a lot of time and energy. It's unlikely to be as bad for the supporter as for the person who's living through the crisis, but it can still wear them down. What's more, they may have commitments of their own to keep going, and their own family members and work colleagues may not have the same underlying concern for, or loyalty to, the person in crisis, and so might resent the amount of effort being put in.

Even where there isn't external pressure to decrease the time and energy someone puts into support, that person will have limits of their own. While the effort may sometimes come to an abrupt halt, it seems to me more as if *sympathy has a half-life*. Those who remember learning physics at school may recall that any radioactive substance will have a particular length of time over which it loses half of its radioactivity; and over the same time period again it will lose half of what's left, and so on, and so on. In loose terms, sympathy seems to work the same way; it doesn't (usually) vanish in an instant but lessens over time, so that while there is usually some residual sympathy, the amount expressed may be quite small. And for many people, that's exactly how they'd prefer it; they don't want always to be looked at sympathetically as the poor person who lost their wife/job/business/home. But when you are looking for support, and it seems to be draining away, it's as well to recognise that's probably the natural order of things.

As sympathy declines, it is often replaced by a simple acceptance of the new reality (as we saw in Chapter 4); but as that may lack some of the trappings of sympathy, it can be mistaken for being uncaring.

## Different kinds of support

There's a final point to make about this whole 'support' business; this word covers some radically different things. We sometimes identify four major categories of support:

- *Emotional support:* this is sometimes the only thing people are thinking of when they say support. It covers things like listening to the person, accepting (or at least tolerating) their tears and outbursts, and trying to do nice things to cheer them up.
- *Informational support:* not an elegant phrase, certainly, but an important type of help. This means giving a person the information that will help them cope better – explaining what has happened, suggestions of things that might help, telling people where else they can turn.
- *Practical support:* actual, tangible help, such as doing tasks for the person, fixing things, lending them money and so on.
- *Social support:* although it can overlap with emotional support, in its purest form this is about knowing you're not alone; either by just having friends or (stronger still) mixing with others who are 'in the same boat'.

The reason for spelling out these different types of support is that, sometimes, the problem is not that others aren't being supportive, it's just that the type of support they're offering isn't the type you need. I always remember this from a family I was supporting some years ago; the mother (call her Carol), in her early forties, had advanced cancer and no longer had the strength or energy to do much of the work of caring for the children. We were able to work out that she was best concentrating on listening to the children, reading stories and even just watching TV with them. Her husband Gary was left with caring for her physical needs, holding down the job that was now their main source of income (and would be vital after her death) as well as all the practicalities of raising a family. During one meeting he told me about a Sunday evening when his wife had gone to bed early feeling ill and exhausted; he was struggling to get the children to have baths, pack their schoolbags and go upstairs at a reasonable hour, and being aware that he had packed lunches to make, and a fortnight's laundry around him including the children's school uniforms for the next day. Just then a very kindly neighbour came round to see how things were. As Carol was in bed, she sat down to see how Gary was doing; as much as he appreciated her concern, Gary told me how throughout the conversation he was getting more and more frantic about all the things he'd still have to do after she left. He said that the worst moment was when she said, 'I just want you to know that, whatever you're going through, I'm there for you.' Being a polite chap, he said, 'Thank you, that means a lot to both of us'; what he wanted to say – or possibly shout – was 'I DON'T WANT YOU TO BE THERE FOR ME – I WANT YOU TO DO MY IRONING!'

The key point was that she was generously offering emotional support, but at that particular moment he needed practical support more than anything else. But when we discussed the incident further, Gary realised that this particular neighbour, being genuinely motivated to help, would probably have been more than happy to help with ironing; as a parent and grandparent she understood some of the pressures, and (like many friends in these situations) felt basically helpless in the face of a tragic situation. People often appreciate a concrete task that visibly helps out. Obviously not everyone is able to help in every way, and we have to take care that people don't feel exploited or taken for granted. But the principle does often apply; when someone is trying to be supportive, you can try to shape the kind of support if necessary.

---

**Try this now:**

Think of a problem that someone you know has been dealing with (e.g. illness, divorce, work stress) and try to think of as many examples as possible of the different kinds of support someone could offer them:

- emotional
- informational
- practical
- social.

Now consider your own current difficulties; think about what kinds of support you have received:

- emotional
- informational
- practical
- social.

If any of those categories are missing, try to consider whether that's because you don't feel the need for that type of support, whether you've not felt able to accept it, or whether it's not been available. And if it's not been available so far, what's your plan for going out there to find it?

But not all of us find it easy to ask for things; a good principle is to try to be clear with the other person about what your situation is, the kind of help you therefore need (and maybe how it will help). Some would then add a pause to see whether an offer was forthcoming, before making a polite but clear enquiry about whether the other person was able to help out. So, in Gary's case above, he might have said:

'Thanks for being willing to help. Actually, the biggest problem at the moment is that, with Carol so weak, I'm having to keep the house, the kids and my job going as well as looking after her. If someone was just able to lend a hand with some of the practical things – a bit of ironing or shopping – it'd actually make a big difference to us all. Is there any chance you could help out a bit that way?'

It might feel a bit odd asking so directly for help, but if someone is offering support, it's fair enough to find out whether they can offer the kind of support you need.

Ultimately, a new life forms. Some aspects of it will no doubt be worse than the old, pre-disaster life; there may well be some aspects of it that are, even in a small way, better. But it will certainly be different, and the chances are that you will get used to it, though you should be aware of the risk of feeling guilty about getting on with that new life.

## Which way now?

And what will that new life be like? As the whole premise of this book suggests, some important elements of it will be outside your control. But not all aspects: even when you can't choose what your external circumstances are, you still have choices over what you want to be 'about', how you want to approach life, and what kind of person you want to be.

I hope that way of talking now sounds familiar, because we're back to the sort of Values we looked at in Chapter 9.

If we find ourselves in the position of trying to (or having to) get a fresh start in life, then identifying our Values becomes especially useful.

In every area of life (relationships, work, social life, leisure), we have to choose where we'll put our efforts and what we'll prioritise. The danger is that we can drift towards what seems easiest or most attractive in the moment. And that might pay off in the short term, but the risk is that further down the line this succession of 'line-of-least-resistance' decisions leaves you in a position that you wouldn't have chosen, such as spending too much time on work rather than family.

The alternative is to be clearer about your Values across all those areas of life, and then use those to inform your choices about what you do.

Crucially, these Values will be different for different people; I once met someone who knew he would die soon. He said to me:

'You know the one about "no one says on their deathbed that they wish they'd spent more time at the office"? Well, I do. I had good opportunities, a job I enjoyed and that could have provided well for my family. But I never took it seriously enough – I put in the bare minimum or less, and was a real clock-watcher. So the career didn't advance, I only got the more boring jobs which didn't earn, weren't secure and didn't give any sense of achievement. It didn't do me or my family any good. So actually, I *do* wish I'd spent more time at the office.'

So the key Values that he found he hadn't lived by were around 'being a good provider', and 'sense of personal achievement'. Whether we agree with him or not, those were his Values and he regretted not having lived by them. These things are often only realised in hindsight ('Hang on, this isn't where I wanted to be at this stage of my life').

But why wait for hindsight and regret? If we identify our Values (What matters to me? What do I want my life to be about?) here and now, it can guide our decisions, and put us into a position to take committed action in the service of those Values. Because one could argue that a life lived in accordance with your own Values (whatever they are, wherever they come from) will have more fulfilment and vitality about it than one based entirely on more aimless, case-by-case decisions about what 'feels right'.[101]

So, if you didn't do the 'Find a Value and ACT on it' exercise in Chapter 9, or you did it but haven't followed through on the action part of it, then now might be the perfect time to go back to it!

## Key points

- We can grieve for many other losses in our life beside deaths, and thinking in terms of grief can help us understand how to deal with life after a crisis.
- Reactions to loss or to change for the worse can be extreme, and can swing violently and unpredictably between different states – it can feel as if you're going mad.
- Grief caused by losing someone or something you've loved can have some lifelong effects, as it's not about completely 'letting go' of the thing you've lost, but rather getting used to a different life.
- Grief does change over time, and shouldn't dominate a person's life forever. If it does, it might be worth seeking professional advice.
- For a while, all memories of your life before the event may be painful, or swamped by the feeling of loss; over time, that usually changes, and it generally becomes easier to remember the good times.

- If your life has changed because of the loss of a person, job, or other major part of life, then the new pattern it settles into may differ more from the old one than you expect (see the discussion of four-legged chairs, above).
- Be cautious about major decisions just after a big event; defer those you can, seek advice from those you trust for those you can't put off.
- The support of others may be limited by their under-standing of the situation, by their patience (remember, sympathy has a half-life) and the type of support being offered.
- If someone is offering support, but it's not the kind you need, then you could ask for that ('don't just be there for me, do my ironing').
- Awareness of your own Values can act as a valuable compass, helping you decide in what direction you want to travel, and allowing you to make your choices accordingly.

# 11

# All the different storms

## Conclusion

> Happy families are all alike; every unhappy family is unhappy in its own way.
>
> Leo Tolstoy

What constitutes a happy (or even a contented) time can vary between individuals. But the detail of a disaster probably varies even more. No two divorces, bankruptcies, court cases or illnesses are identical. And there are so many different types of personal disasters that we haven't used as examples here. I hope it hasn't been too great a leap to see how some of the things we use in palliative care apply to other crises; but no matter how specific it aimed to be, no book could ever describe your individual experience precisely.

Similarly, each individual is the sum total of their nature, their past experiences, their thoughts and beliefs and their circumstances; so each reacts differently to events, and will differ also in what helps them best. And that's why this book couldn't simply be a set of instructions, but rather a range of possible techniques some of which will work for one person, others of which will work for another.

Even though details differ, some themes are more common, both in the effects of events and in how to face up to them. And key among those are the two main elements in this book, running alongside each other:

- making sense of what's going on
- finding ways of dealing with it.

Of course, they're not entirely separate; as we saw in Chapter 3, being able to understand what's happening to you is in itself a coping strategy.

On the broader scale, I think we're better equipped to deal with major crises by recognising a truth about life; an uncomfortable truth, but a truth nevertheless. And that is, that alongside the good things in life, there will be some really bad things. Nothing – absolutely *nothing* – that we do can stop every bad thing from happening in our lives. And the best way through is neither to lie down and give up, nor waste our days in wild-goose chases to prevent the inevitable. Instead, we accept and face directly what is happening, make whatever changes we are able to, and make the best we can of whatever hand we're dealt. We might mourn the past – and the future – that we've lost, but there's little to be gained from wasting too much time wishing things were other than they are.

There's an idea about this that goes back at least as far as the emperor-philosopher Marcus Aurelius.[102] It was stated (more concisely) as the Serenity Prayer in the 1930s, and has since been adopted by Alcoholics Anonymous and related programmes. I think that, rephrased slightly, it goes absolutely to the heart of my work in palliative care, and sums up the message of this entire book:

Faced with adversity, we need to find ways:
To change those things that can be changed,
To adjust to those things that can't be changed,
And to tell the difference between the two.

I genuinely believe that the person who applies this test to the serious challenges they meet ('Is this something I can change? And if so how? Or is it something I have to learn to get used to? And if so, how?') will cope better on life's sometimes stormy seas. And the contents of this book should help you to change those things that can be changed, to adjust to the things that can't, and work out which is which.

And what became of the people we've been following?

Peter was made bankrupt, as we know, and served his prison sentence for fraud. We saw how he managed to overcome his sense of shame in front of the people he'd seen as his friends. The limitations put on a bankrupt and his age meant that he was never able to establish another company of his own. He has, though, managed to get some work with an old colleague; he always feels the disappointment over someone else being boss, and (though he'd never admit it to his wife) he always views his working life as having failed. But activity is better than brooding, and the income helps a little towards retirement. His wife feels that, though he is less enthusiastic about work, he is also less obsessed with it, and has more time for her, their son and (she hopes one day) the grandkids.

Debbie continues to be as busy as ever. Her income has gone down because she is doing a less skilled job, and (as she expected) she wasn't able to keep up the mortgage on her house; at least her pragmatism and caution meant that she realised this and acted on it quickly before building up additional debts that she wouldn't be able to pay off. Now she shares a small Housing Association flat with her daughter at the rougher end of the estate. It still hurts that she lost the house; she can't bear going past it, so always takes a slightly longer route to church to avoid it. She's also had to accept that she can't provide her daughter Beccy with everything she would have liked to, but has the satisfaction of seeing her develop at school. She knows Beccy will have to rely more heavily on student loans to see her through college, but hopes that she has instilled enough respect for the value of money in her that she won't see debt as a way of life.

After a very rough few months, Anil finds himself quietly beginning to enjoy life, and particularly the freedom of a single, young urban person with income and friends. There's still loneliness and regret, and a lot of self-doubt about his inability to keep Sarah, but a further year on sees him in another relationship, feeling more secure and confident. In the end, he has even been able to view the loss of Sarah as a narrow escape, as the insecure, uncertain and dependent person he had become with her was not a version of himself that he liked.

And Helen, of course, did die. Well symptom-controlled, with her family around her, but she died nonetheless. Nothing could make that easy for her partner or her children. The grieving is hard, and though a new kind of normal life has eventually established itself, some of that pain carries on for each of them, and will do even when Liam has grown up, and Keith has remarried. And yet, for all the pain, if you were to ask each of the people who knew Helen, and who have felt the pain of grief, 'Would you go back in time, avoid meeting her, and so never feel the pain of losing her?', not one of them would say 'Yes'.

If grief's the price we pay for loving someone, then it is a price worth paying. And Helen would have approved of that.

We cannot avoid all adversity, nor make it all OK; if the storm is coming, then it's coming. The only question is how well we deal with it; and (whether millionaire or pauper) that is what ultimately will define our quality of life.

## Key points

- All crises differ, but there are some things they have in common.
- There is nothing we can do that guarantees bad things will never happen to us.
- Even when bad things are out of our control, the way we choose to react can still make a big difference.
- We need to understand, as best we can, what is happening to us, and find ways that make a difference to it (however small).

- Faced with adversity, we need to find ways:
  - to change those things that can be changed
  - to adjust to those things that can't be changed
  - to tell the difference between the two.
- You can't control the storm, but you can control how you react to it.

# Afterword

I grew up in the North West of England, where it seemed to be wet and windy for months at a time. Caught in yet another cold shower, I'd scurry along hunched forward, face screwed up against the weather. It took a friend from a gentler climate who moved to the area to point something out to me: if you walk upright, face relaxed, the cold and wet aren't any worse. They're still the same; but you feel better.

Next time life throws a storm in your face, try it.

# Further reading and further help

I've included references at points throughout the book, for anyone who wants to check the background and the research relating to some of the things I've said. Before that, though, are some more general texts that might be a good place to start if you want to go further with some of the areas we've covered.

## The psychological impact of cancer

I think the best overall review of this area is:

Brennan, J. with Moynihan, C. (2004) *Cancer in Context: A Practical Guide to Supportive Care*, Oxford, Oxford University Press.

For practical advice on maintaining a sense of control, especially in the early stages of cancer, I'd suggest:

Dainow, S., Golding, V. and Wright, J. (2001) *44½ Choices You Can Make If You Have Cancer*, Dublin, Newleaf.

For other aspects of cancer, I wouldn't recommend a book, but rather a website as a starting point – that started by the Cancerbackup charity and now continued by Macmillan Cancer Relief. It provides up-to-date, reputable, and reliable information on many aspects of cancer in all its forms:

www.macmillan.org.uk

## The psychology of thinking (including decision-making)

I am afraid I don't know any 'light' reading books on this topic; a good general introduction might be a textbook, for example:

Eysenck, M. and Keane, M. (2010) *Cognitive Psychology: A Student's Handbook*, 6th edn, London, Psychology Press.

Specifically on decision-making, the going gets tougher still; the following book is excellent, but fairly academic:

Baron, J. (2007) *Thinking and Deciding*, 4th edn, Cambridge, Cambridge University Press.

## Cognitive therapy and cognitive behavioural therapy

There are several books giving an overview; unless your interest is very theoretical, you might get the best feel from books aimed at clients and patients. One of the best is:

Padesky, C. and Greenberger, D. (1995) *Mind Over Mood: Change How You Feel by Changing the Way You Think*, New York, Guilford.

For something more specific to particular problems, there is the 'Overcoming' series, which is a number of self-help guides for different specific psychological issues using cognitive behavioural methods, and written by leading UK-based psychologists or psychotherapists. For example:

Fennell, M. J. V. (2009) *Overcoming Low Self-Esteem*, London, Robinson.
Gilbert, P. (2009) *Overcoming Depression*, London, Robinson.

## Mindfulness and acceptance

For mindfulness-based stress reduction, the classic text, and still a good starting place, is:

Kabat-Zinn, J. (1991) *Full Catastrophe Living: How to Cope with Stress, Pain and Illness Using Mindfulness Meditation*, London, Piatkus.

Another popular introduction is applicable to a much wider range of problems than the title suggests and includes a CD of mindfulness practices led by Jon Kabat-Zinn:

Williams, J. M. G., Segal, Z. V., Teasdale, J. D. and Kabat-Zinn, J. (2007) *The Mindful Way through Depression*, New York, Guilford.

The University of Bangor is home to the Centre for Mindfulness Research and Practice, a mindfulness research centre, and maintains a website with up-to-date links and references if you want to delve further:

www.bangor.ac.uk/mindfulness

## Acceptance and commitment therapy

Good, wide-ranging self-help books for this approach are:

Hayes, S. (2005) *Get out of Your Mind and into Your Life*, Oakland, CA, New Harbinger Press.
Harris, R. (2008) *The Happiness Trap*, London, Robinson.

There's also a very good website linked to this text:

www.thehappinesstrap.com

## Compassionate mind training

Try reading one of Paul Gilbert's books on the subject, for example:

Gilbert, P. (2009) *The Compassionate Mind*, London, Constable & Robinson.

## Finding a therapist or a counsellor

If you decide you need some professional support with all this, then the best first step might be to talk to your health or social care providers (e.g. your GP).

If you decide to seek private help, check out the registers maintained by the reputable professional organisations. Three of the key ones are:

- British Association for Counselling and Psychotherapy
  www.bacp.co.uk
- British Association for Behavioural and Cognitive Psychotherapies
  www.babcp.com
- British Psychological Society, though their register also includes people from other branches of psychology (e.g. teachers of psychology and researchers), so read the entries carefully:
  www.bps.org.uk

Other specific therapies are likely to have their own regulating bodies, which may well maintain a list of practitioners on their own websites. Although there aren't as many therapists using ACT (yet) as some other approaches, they can be found here:

www.contextualpsychology.org

Although most of these resources are obviously UK-based, the basic strategy (talk to health and social care providers, look at the databases of the professional organisations) should still pay off wherever you live.

# References

1 Weinberg, J. and Levine, S. (1980) 'Psychobiology of coping in animals: The effects of predictability', in S. Levine and H. Ursin (eds) *Coping and Health*, New York, Plenum.

2 Cicero (trans.) *Tusculan Disputations*, Online, Project Gutenberg, available www.gutenberg.org/ebooks/14988 (accessed 31 December 2010).

3 Kim, S. Y. H., Holloway, R. G., Frank, S., Wilson, R. and Kieburtz, K. (2008) 'Trust in early phase research: Therapeutic optimism and protective pessimism', *Medicine, Health Care and Philosophy*, 11(4), 393–401.

4 Epictetus (trans.) *The Enchiridion*, Online, Project Gutenberg, available www.gutenberg.org/ebooks/10661 (accessed 31 December 2010).

5 Hawkins, S. A. and Hastie, R. (1990) 'Hindsight: Biased judgments of past events after the outcomes are known', *Psychological Bulletin*, 107, 311–327.

6 Buckman, R. A. (2005) 'Breaking bad news: The S-P-I-K-E-S strategy', *Community Oncology*, 2, 138–142.

7 Ptacek, J. T. and Eberhardt, T. L. (1996) 'Breaking bad news: A review of the literature', *Journal of the American Medical Association*, 276, 496–502.

8 Kübler-Ross, E. (1973) *On Death and Dying*, London, Routledge.

9 Tooby, J. and Cosmides, L. (1990) 'The past explains the present: Emotional adaptations and the structure of ancestral environments', *Ethology and Sociobiology*, 11, 375–424.

10  Hayes, S. C., Strosahl, K. and Wilson, K. G. (1999) *Acceptance and Commitment Therapy: An Experimental Approach to Behavior Change*, New York, Guilford.

11  Carlick, A. and Biley, F. (2004) 'Thoughts on the therapeutic use of narrative in the promotion of coping in cancer care', *European Journal of Cancer Care*, 13, 308–317.

12  Leventhal, H., Meyer, D. and Nerenz, D. R. (1980) 'The common sense representation of illness danger', in S. Rachman (ed.) *Contributions to Medical Psychology, Volume 2*, New York, Pergamon, pp. 17–30.

13  Kipling, R. (1902/1987) *The Jungle Book*, London, Puffin, p. 70.

14  Brennan, J. (2001) 'Adjustment to cancer: Coping or personal transition?', *Psycho-Oncology*, 10, 1–18.

15  Marcus Aurelius (trans.) *Meditations*, Online, Project Gutenberg, available www.gutenberg.org/ebooks/2680 (accessed 31 December 2010).

16  Butow, P. N., Brown, R. F., Cogar, S., Tattersall, M. H. and Dunn S. M. (2002) 'Oncologists' reactions to cancer patients' verbal cues', *Psycho-Oncology*, 11, 47–58.

17  Miller, S. M. (1987) 'Monitoring and blunting: Validation of a questionnaire to assess styles of information seeking under threat', *Journal of Personality and Social Psychology*, 52, 345–353.

18  Salkovskis, P. M. and Warwick, M. C. (1986) 'Morbid preoccupations, health anxiety and reassurance: A cognitive-behavioural approach to hypochondriasis', *Behaviour Research and Therapy*, 24, 597–602.

19  Hart, W., Albarracín, D., Eagly, A. H., Brechan, I., Lindberg, M. J. and Merrill, L. (2009) 'Feeling validated versus being correct: A meta-analysis of selective exposure to information', *Psychological Bulletin*, 135, 555–588.

20  Stokes, J. A. (2000) *The Secret C: Straight Talking about Cancer*, London, Winston's Wish/Macmillan Cancer Relief.

21  Kübler-Ross, E. (1973) *On Death and Dying*, London, Routledge.

22  Parkes, C. M. (1970) 'The first year of bereavement: A longitudinal study of the reaction of London widows to the death of their husbands', *Psychiatry*, 33, 444–467.

23 Chesters, S., Owen, R. and Skevington, S. (2005) 'Making sense of "adjustment to cancer": Views of specialist palliative care nurses', *Proceedings of the British Psychological Society*, 13, 65–66.

24 Lazarus, R. S. and Folkman, S. (1984) *Stress, Appraisal, and Coping*, New York, Springer, pp. 171–174.

25 Padesky, C. A. (1994) 'Schema change processes in cognitive therapy', *Clinical Psychology and Psychotherapy*, 1, 267–278.

26 Brennan, J. (2001) 'Adjustment to cancer: Coping or personal transition?', *Psycho-Oncology*, 10, 1–18.

27 Seligman, M. E. P. (1975) *Helplessness: On Depression, Development, and Death*, San Francisco, CA, W. H. Freeman.

28 Breznitz, S. (1983) 'The seven kinds of denial', in S. Breznitz (ed.) *The Denial of Stress*, New York, International Universities Press, pp. 257–278.

29 Trunnell, E. E. and Holt, W. E. (1974) 'The concept of denial or disavowal', *Journal of the American Psychoanalytic Association*, 22, 769–784.

30 Brennan, J. (2001) 'Adjustment to cancer: Coping or personal transition?', *Psycho-Oncology*, 10, 1–18.

31 Miller, W. R. and Rollnick, S. (2002) *Motivational Interviewing: Preparing People for Change*, New York, Guilford, pp. 98–111.

32 Ende, J., Kazis, L., Ash, A. and Moskowitz, M. A. (1989) 'Measuring patients' desire for autonomy: Decision making and information-seeking preferences among medical patients', *Journal of General Internal Medicine*, 4, 23–30.

33 Jianakoplos, N. A. and Bernasek, A. (1998) 'Are women more risk averse?', *Economic Inquiry*, 36, 620–630.

34 Ajzen, I. (1985) 'From intentions to actions: A theory of planned behavior', in J. Kuhl and J. Beckmann (eds) *Action-Control: From Cognition to Behaviour*, Heidelberg, Springer, pp. 11–39.

35 Gilovich, T. and Griffin, D. (2002) 'Heuristics and biases – then and now', in T. Gilovich, D. Griffin and D. Kahneman (eds) *Heuristics and Biases: The Psychology of Intuitive Judgment*, Cambridge, Cambridge University Press, pp. 1–18.

36  Dijksterhuis, A. and Nordgren, L. F. (2006) 'A theory of unconscious thought', *Perspectives on Psychological Science*, 1, 95–109.

37  Tversky, A. and Kahneman, D. (1974) 'Judgment under uncertainty: Heuristics and biases', *Science*, 185, 1124–1131.

38  Simon, H. A. (1956) 'Rational choice and the structure of the environment', *Psychological Review*, 63, 129–138.

39  Grzybowska, P. and Finlay, I. (1997) 'The incidence of suicide in palliative care patients', *Palliative Medicine*, 11, 313–316.

40  General Medical Council (GMC) (2010) *Treatment and Care Towards the End of Life: Good Practice in Decision Making*, London, GMC, p. 20.

41  Bhagat, R. S. (1983) 'Effects of stressful life events on individual performance effectiveness and work adjustment processes within organizational settings', *Academy of Management Review*, 8, 660–671.

42  Cohen, S. and Hoberman, H. M. (1983) 'Positive events and social supports as buffers of life change stress', *Journal of Applied Psychology*, 13, 99–125.

43  Watters, E. (2004) *Urban Tribes: Are Friends the New Family?*, London, Bloomsbury.

44  Hodges, L. G., Humphris, G. M. and Macfarlane, G. (2005) 'A meta-analytic investigation of the relationship between the psychological distress of cancer patients and their carers', *Social Science and Medicine*, 60, 1–12.

45  Chalmers, A. (2009) *When a Parent is Terminally Ill: Supporting Children*, London, Child Bereavement Charity.

46  Salmon, P. (2001) 'Effects of physical exercise on anxiety, depression, and sensitivity to stress: A unifying theory', *Clinical Psychology Review*, 21, 33–61.

47  Vanage, S. M., Gilbertson, K. K. and Mathiowetz, V. (2003) 'Effects of an energy conservation course on fatigue impact for persons with progressive multiple sclerosis', *American Journal of Occupational Therapy*, 57, 315–323.

48  Brewin, C. R., Andrews, B. and Rose, S. (2000) 'Fear, helplessness, and horror in posttraumatic stress disorder: Investigating DSM-IV Criterion A2 in victims of violent crime', *Journal of Traumatic Stress*, 13, 499–509.

49 Simonson, I. (1992) 'The influence of anticipating regret and responsibility on purchase decisions', *Journal of Consumer Research*, 19, 105–118.

50 Williams, C. J. (2003) *Overcoming Anxiety: A Five Areas Approach*, London, Arnold.

51 Gross, J. J. and Levenson, R. W. (1997) 'Hiding feelings: The acute effects of inhibiting negative and positive emotion', *Journal of Abnormal Psychology*, 106, 95–103.

52 Owen, R. and Jeffrey, D. (2008) 'Communication: Common challenging scenarios in cancer care', *European Journal of Cancer*, 44, 1163–1168.

53 Lavender, A. and Watkins, E. (2004) 'Rumination and future thinking in depression', *British Journal of Clinical Psychology*, 43, 129–142.

54 Stratton, V. N. and Zalanowski, A. H. (1991) 'The effects of music and cognition on mood', *Psychology of Music*, 19, 121–127.

55 Sheslow, D. V. and Erickson, M. T. (1975) 'Analysis of activity preference in depressed and nondepressed college students', *Journal of Counselling Psychology*, 22, 329–332.

56 Hopko, D. R., Lejuez, C. W., Ruggiero, K. J. and Eifert, G. H. (2003) 'Contemporary behavioral activation treatments for depression: Procedures, principles, and progress', *Clinical Psychology Review*, 23, 699–717.

57 Beck, A. T., Rush, A. J., Shaw, B. F. and Emery, G. (1979) *Cognitive Therapy of Depression*, New York, Guilford.

58 Nabkasorn, C., Miyai, N., Sootmongkol, A., Junprasert, S., Yamamoto, H., Arita, M. and Miyashita, K. (2006) 'Effects of physical exercise on depression, neuroendocrine stress hormones and physiological fitness in adolescent females with depressive symptoms', *European Journal of Public Health*, 16, 179–184.

59 Butler, A. C., Chapman, J. E., Forman, E. M. and Beck, A. T. (2006) 'The empirical status of cognitive-behavioral therapy: A review of meta-analyses', *Clinical Psychology Review*, 26, 17–31.

60 Hayes, S. C., Strosahl, K. and Wilson, K. G. (1999) *Acceptance and Commitment Therapy: An Experiential Approach to Behavior Change*, New York, Guilford.

61 Mol, S. L., Arntz, A. M., Job, F. M., Dinant, G., Vilters-Van Montfort, A. P. and Knottnerus, J. A. (2005) 'Symptoms of post-traumatic stress disorder after non-traumatic events: Evidence from an open population study', *British Journal of Psychiatry*, 186, 494–499.

62 Beck, J. S. (1995) *Cognitive Therapy: Basics and Beyond*, New York, Guilford.

63 Bracha, H. S., Ralston, T. C., Matsukawa, J. M., Williams, A. E. and Bracha, S. (2004) 'Does "fight or flight" need updating?', *Psychosomatics*, 45, 448–449.

64 Harris, R. (2006) 'Embracing your demons: An overview of acceptance and commitment therapy', *Psychotherapy in Australia*, 12, 3–10.

65 Schlinger, H. D. (1996) 'How the human got its spots: A critical analysis of the Just So Stories of evolutionary biology', *Skeptic*, 4, 68–76.

66 Watkins, E., Moulds, M. and Mackintosh, B. (2005) 'Comparisons between rumination and worry in a non-clinical population', *Behaviour Research and Therapy*, 12, 1577–1585.

67 Leahy, R. L. (2006) *The Worry Cure: Seven Steps to Stop Worry from Stopping You*, New York, Three Rivers Press.

68 Kabat-Zinn, J. (2004) *Wherever You Go, There You Are*, London, Piatkus.

69 Csikszentmihalyi, M. (2002) *Flow: The Psychology of Happiness*, New York, Rider.

70 Jeffrey, D., Jeffrey, P., Jones, D. and Owen, R. (2001) 'Un cours pratique et innovateur sur l'art pour les professionnels de santé', *Le Journal Européen de Soins Palliatifs*, 8, 203–206.

71 Jin, P. (1992) 'Efficacy of Tai Chi, brisk walking, meditation, and reading in reducing mental and emotional stress', *Journal of Psychosomatic Research*, 36, 361–370.

72 Hoffart, M. B. and Keene, E. P. (1998) 'Body–mind–spirit: The benefits of visualization', *American Journal of Nursing*, 98, 44–47.

73 Flammer, E. and Bongartz, W. (2003) 'On the efficacy of hypnosis: A meta-analytic study', *Contemporary Hypnosis*, 20, 179–197.

74 Walsh, R. and Shapiro, S. L. (2006) 'The meeting of meditative disciplines and western psychology: A mutually enriching dialogue', *American Psychologist*, 61, 227–239.

75 Adler, C. M., Craske, M. G. and Barlow, D. H. (1987) 'Relaxation-Induced Panic (RIP): When resting isn't peaceful', *Integrative Psychiatry*, 5, 94–100.

76 Ax, A. F. (1953) 'The physiological differentiation between fear and anger in humans', *Psychosomatic Medicine*, 15, 433–442.

77 Callaghan, P. (2004) 'Exercise: A neglected intervention in mental health care?', *Journal of Psychiatric and Mental Health Nursing*, 11, 476–483.

78 Baumeister, R. F., Stillwell, A. M. and Heatherton, T. F. (1994) 'Guilt: An interpersonal approach', *Psychological Bulletin*, 115, 243–267.

79 Alcoholics Anonymous (2001) *Alcoholics Anonymous*, 4th edn, New York, Alcoholics Anonymous World Services.

80 Tangney, J. P., Miller, R. S., Flicker, L. and Barlow, D. H. (1996) 'Are shame, guilt, and embarrassment distinct emotions?', *Journal of Personality and Social Psychology*, 70, 1256–1269.

81 Gilbert, P. (2009) *The Compassionate Mind*, London, Constable & Robinson.

82 Lazarus, R. S. (1999) 'Hope: An emotion and a vital coping resource against despair', *Social Research*, 66, 653–678.

83 Schofield, P., Ball, D. and Smith, J. G. (2004) 'Optimism and survival in lung carcinoma patients', *Cancer*, 100, 1276–1282.

84 Everson, S. A., Goldberg, D. E., Kaplan, G. A., Cohen, R. D., Pukkala, E., Tuomilehto, J. and Salonen, J. T. (1996) 'Hopelessness and risk of mortality and incidence of myocardial infarction and cancer', *Psychosomatic Medicine*, 58, 113–121.

85 Benzein, E., Norberg, A. and Saveman, B. (2001) 'The meaning of the lived experience of hope in patients with cancer in palliative home care', *Palliative Medicine*, 15, 117–126.

86 Thuné-Boyle, I. C., Stygall, J. A., Keshtgar, M. R. and Newman, S. P. (2006) 'Do religious/spiritual coping strategies affect illness adjustment in patients with cancer? A systematic review of the literature', *Social Science and Medicine*, 63, 151–164.

87 James, O. (2007) *Affluenza*, London, Vermilion.

88 Grossman, P., Niemann, L., Schmidt, S. and Walach, H. (2004) 'Mindfulness-based stress reduction and health benefits. A meta-analysis', *Journal of Psychosomatic Research*, 57, 35–43.

89 Morone, N. E., Greco, C. M. and Weiner, D. K. (2008) 'Mindfulness meditation for the treatment of chronic low back pain in older adults: A randomized controlled pilot study', *Pain*, 134, 310–319.

90 Grossman, P., Kappos, L., Gensicke, H., D'Souza, M., Mohr, D. C., Penner, I. K. and Steiner, C. (2010) 'MS quality of life, depression, and fatigue improve after mindfulness training: A randomized trial', *Neurology*, 75, 1141–1149.

91 Teasdale, J. D., Segal, Z. V. and Williams, J. M. G. (2000) 'Prevention of relapse/recurrence in major depression by Mindfulness-Based Cognitive Therapy', *Journal of Consulting and Clinical Psychology*, 68, 615–623.

92 Shennan, C., Payne, S. and Fenlon, D. (2010) 'What is the evidence for the use of mindfulness-based interventions in cancer care? A review', *Psycho-Oncology*, available http://onlinelibrary.wiley.com/doi/10.1002/pon.1819/ (accessed 13 February 2011).

93 Carlson, L. E. and Garland, S. N. (2005) 'Impact of mindfulness-based stress reduction (MBSR) on sleep, mood, stress and fatigue symptoms in cancer outpatients', *International Journal of Behavioral Medicine*, 12, 278–285.

94 Killingsworth, M. A. and Gilbert, D. T. (2010) 'A wandering mind is an unhappy mind', *Science*, 330, 932.

95 Harris, R. (2009) *ACT Made Simple*, Oakland, CA, New Harbinger, p. 191.

96 Ruiz, F. J. (2010) 'A review of Acceptance and Commitment Therapy (ACT) empirical evidence: Correlational, experimental psychopathology, component and outcome studies', *International Journal of Psychology and Psychological Therapy*, 10, 125–162.

97 Carnelly, K. B., Wortman, C. B., Bolger, N. and Burke, C. T. (2006) 'The time course of grief reactions to spousal loss: Evidence from a national probability sample', *Journal of Personality and Social Psychology*, 91, 476–492.

98  Stroebe, M. and Schut, H. (1999) 'The dual process model of coping with bereavement: Rationale and description', *Death Studies*, 23, 197–224.

99  Klass, D., Silverman, P. R. and Nickman, R. (eds) (1996) *Continuing Bonds: New Understandings of Grief*, London, Taylor & Francis.

100  Goldenberg, I. and Goldenberg, H. (2008) *Family Therapy: An Overview*, Belmont, CA, Thomson Brooks/Cole.

101  Hayes, S. C., Luoma, J. B., Bond, F. W., Masuda, A. and Lillis, J. (2006) 'Acceptance and Commitment Therapy: Model, processes and outcomes', *Behaviour Research and Therapy*, 44, 1–25.

102  Marcus Aurelius (trans.) *Meditations*, Online, Project Gutenberg, available www.gutenberg.org/ebooks/2680 (accessed 31 December 2010).

# Index